D1643789

T H E   B O O K   O F

Light
PASTA SAUCES

THE BOOK OF

Light
PASTA SAUCES

ANNE SHEASBY

Photographed by
SIMON BUTCHER

PUBLISHED BY
SALAMANDER BOOKS LIMITED
LONDON

Published by Salamander Books Limited
8 Blenheim Court, Brewery Road, London N7 9NT, United Kingdom

9 8 7 6 5 4 3 2

© Salamander Books Ltd., 1995

ISBN 0-86101-783-8

Produced by ZEBU
Editor: Vicky Hanson
Art Director: Vicky Zentner
Photographer: Simon Butcher
Photographer's Assistant: Giles Stokoe
Home Economist: Justine Dickenson
Home Economist's Assistant: Liz Comben
Stylist: Jo Mason
Colour separation: Classic Scan Pte. Ltd., Singapore
Printed and bound in Spain by Bookprint, S.L.

ACKNOWLEDGEMENTS
The publishers would like to thank the following for their help:
Meyer (UK) Ltd. for supplying the saucepans
Liberty and John Lewis for the loan of their china

Notes:
All spoon measurements are level.
1 teaspoon = 5 ml spoon.
1 tablespoon = 15 ml spoon.

CONTENTS

INTRODUCTION

Pasta was once thought to be high in calories and therefore a 'fattening' food to be avoided. Nothing could be further from the truth. Pasta is, in fact, a highly nutritious food - it is an excellent source of carbohydrate and provides protein, dietary fibre, vitamins and minerals. It is low in fat and is a valuable source of energy, providing a nourishing, easily digestible meal.

The sauces served with pasta are usually responsible for piling on the fat and calories, but with careful selection of ingredients, and replacing the more traditional ones, such as cream and butter, with lighter alternatives, you'll be able to create healthy yet delicious pasta sauces that are low in fat and calories.

The Book of Light Pasta Sauces gives recipes for sauces containing meat, poultry, fish and shellfish, vegetables, and eggs and cheese, all illustrated in full colour, with step-by-step instructions and calorie and fat levels for quick, easy reference.

─── COOKING WITH PASTA ───

Pasta is traditionally associated with Italy and has played an important role in the Italian diet for centuries. Yet egg and rice noodles also form a part of the staple diet of many Asian countries and some people believe pasta actually originated in China. Today, however, pasta is a popular food all over the world, and the range of fresh and dried pastas available in supermarkets and delicatessens is considerable.

VARIETIES OF PASTA

The word pasta literally means 'dough', and this dough is a basic mixture of wheat flour and water, to which flavourings and colourings are often added. Most dried pasta is a pale yellow colour. Pasta which has eggs added to the basic mixture is a darker yellow and is known as *pasta all'uova*. *Pasta verde* is flavoured with spinach to give it a green colour; *pasta rossa* has tomato purée added to make it a pale reddish orange. Other, less common, colours of pasta available include black (coloured with squid ink), pale brown (flavoured with chocolate or mushrooms), deep pink (coloured with beetroot), and deep yellow (coloured with saffron). The darker brown varieties of wholewheat and buckwheat pasta contain more fibre than the other types of pasta and have a chewier texture. Filled pastas, such as ravioli and tortellini, traditionally contain stuffings of ground meats or a classic mixture of spinach and cheese.

Home-made pasta is becoming more popular and is relatively easy to make, particularly with the help of a pasta-making machine, which both kneads and rolls the dough for you. Home-made pasta is made from a simple mixture of flour, salt, oil and water or eggs. The best flour to use is semolina flour but this is quite difficult to obtain, so strong breadmaking flour may be used instead. The high gluten content of the strong flour makes the dough easier to knead and roll out.

PASTA SHAPES

Each recipe in this book recommends the most suitable type of pasta for that particular sauce, but there are no strict rules and you can mix and match as you like. On the right are some of the varieties you can choose from.

Spaghetti
Long, thin, string-like strands.

Spaghettini
Thin spaghetti.

Tagliatelle
Long, flat, ribbon-like strands.

Tagliarini
Thin tagliatelle.

Fettucine
Long, thin, flat ribbons, slightly narrower than tagliatelle.

Linguine
Similar to spaghetti but slightly fatter.

Vermicelli
Long, thin strands.

Bucatini
Long, thin, hollow pasta.

Fusilli
Short, spiral-shaped.

Conchiglie
Shell-shaped.

Farfalle
Butterfly or bow-shaped.

Penne
Quill-shaped pasta tubes, ridged (*rigate*) or smooth.

Rigatoni
Short, fat, ridged tubes.

Ravioli
Filled squares of pasta.

Tortellini
Filled, curled semi-circles of pasta.

Pipe rigate
Curved, short, ridged tubes.

Lasagnette
Flat strips of pasta with wavy edges.

Fusilli bucati
Corkscrew twists.

Macaroni
Short, hollow tubes.

STORING PASTA

Dried pasta should be stored in a dry, dark place, where it will keep for up to 2 years. Fresh pasta has a much shorter shelf-life and must be kept in the refrigerator, for no longer than 3 days. Fresh pasta can be frozen and stored for up to 3 months. Layered or filled pasta, such as lasagne or ravioli, also freezes well, but cooked pasta frozen in a sauce tends to become too soft when thawed.

COOKING PASTA

Pasta should always be cooked in a large pan containing plenty of fast-boiling water: 2-3 litres (3½-5 pints) per 450 g (1 lb) of pasta. You can add 1-2 teaspoons of salt or lemon juice to the cooking water for extra flavour. A teaspoon of oil added to the pan when the water is boiling will prevent the pasta from sticking together.

Once the water has reached a fast boil, add the pasta, stirring to separate it. Return the water to the boil, calculating the cooking time from the moment a rolling boil is reached. Leave the pan uncovered and stir the pasta occasionally.

Cooking times vary according to the type of pasta so it is always best to follow the guidelines on the packet. Dried unfilled pasta usually cooks in 8-12 minutes, and dried filled pasta in 15-20 minutes. Fresh unfilled pasta takes 2-3 minutes and fresh filled pasta 7-10 minutes. Cooked pasta should be *al dente* (literally, 'to the tooth') which means the pasta should be firm to the bite. As soon as the pasta is cooked, remove from the heat and drain in a colander or sieve. Do not rinse it.

Frozen fresh pasta does not need to be thawed before cooking.

QUANTITIES OF PASTA

In Italy, pasta is traditionally served as a starter, but most of the recipes in this book are intended to be served as a main course. For a main meal, allow 85-115 g (3-4 oz) of dried pasta per person, or 115-150 g (4-5 oz) of fresh.

NUTRITIONAL CONTENT

The pasta given as serving suggestions in this book is not included in the calorie counts and fat figures at the end of each recipe.

When cooked, 25 g (1 oz) of dried pasta contains:
Cals/Kj: 94/398
Fat: 0.6 g

BEEF & OYSTER

70 ml (2 ½ fl oz/ ⅓ cup) red wine
2 tablespoons dark soy sauce
2 tablespoons oyster sauce
2 cloves garlic, crushed
450 g (1 lb) lean rump steak, cut into thin strips
2 teaspoons sunflower oil
2.5 cm (1 in) piece fresh root ginger, peeled and
 finely chopped
1 bunch spring onions, cut into 1 cm (½ in) lengths
1 red pepper (capsicum), sliced
3 carrots, cut into matchstick strips
1 tablespoon cornflour
150 ml (5 fl oz/ ⅔ cup) beef stock
salt and freshly ground black pepper
flat-leaf parsley, to garnish

In a bowl, mix together the red wine, soy sauce, oyster sauce and garlic. Add the steak and stir until the meat is coated with the marinade. Cover, chill and leave to marinate for 1 hour. In a large frying pan or wok, heat the oil. Remove the meat from the marinade with a slotted spoon, reserving the marinade, and add the meat to the pan with the ginger, spring onions, pepper (capsicum) and carrots. Stir-fry the meat and vegetables over a high heat for 3-5 minutes, until the meat is browned and cooked through.

In a bowl, blend the cornflour with the stock and marinade and add to the pan with the salt and pepper. Bring to the boil over a high heat, stirring continuously for 1-2 minutes, until the sauce is thickened and glossy. Garnish with flat-leaf parsley and serve immediately with freshly cooked spaghetti.

Serves 6. Makes 1.1 litres (38 ½ fl oz/5 cups).

Total Cals/Kj: 983/4124   Total fat: 33.0 g
Cals/Kj per portion: 164/687   Fat per portion: 5.5 g
Cals/Kj per cup: 207/868   Fat per cup: 6.9 g

SMOKED HAM & LEEK

25 g (1 oz/2 tablespoons) half fat spread
450 g (1 lb) leeks, sliced
25 g (1 oz/ ¼ cup) plain flour
300 ml (10 fl oz/1 ¼ cups) semi-skimmed milk
4 tablespoons pork or vegetable stock
225 g (8 oz) lean cooked smoked ham, diced
1 teaspoon dried sage
salt and freshly ground black pepper
2 tablespoons reduced fat single (light) cream
fresh sage, to garnish

In a saucepan, melt the half fat spread over a
low heat. Add the leeks and cook gently
for 8 minutes, stirring occasionally.

Stir in the flour and cook for 1 minute,
stirring. Remove the pan from the heat and
gradually stir in the milk and stock. Bring
slowly to the boil, stirring, and continue to
cook, stirring, until the mixture thickens.

Add the ham, sage and salt and pepper and
simmer gently for 5 minutes, stirring.
Remove the pan from the heat and stir in the
cream. Garnish with sage and serve with
freshly cooked fettucine.

Serves 4. Makes 850 ml (30 fl oz/3¾ cups).

Total Cals/Kj: 738/3101   Total fat: 32.5 g
Cals/Kj per portion: 185/775   Fat per portion: 8.1 g
Cals/Kj per cup: 197/827   Fat per cup: 8.7 g

Variation: Use smoked chicken in place of
the smoked ham.

CHILLI MINCED BEEF

1 teaspoon olive oil
1 large onion, chopped
1 red pepper (capsicum), diced
1 clove garlic, crushed
450 g (1 lb) extra lean minced beef
225 g (8 oz) can chopped tomatoes
400 g (14 oz) can red kidney beans, rinsed and
   drained
150 ml (5 fl oz/⅔ cup) beef stock
2 tablespoons tomato purée (paste)
3 tablespoons dry sherry
2 teaspoons hot chilli powder
1 teaspoon dried mixed herbs
½ teaspoon ground cumin
salt and freshly ground black pepper
parsley sprigs, to garnish

In a large pan, heat the oil and cook the onion, red pepper (capsicum) and garlic for 3 minutes. Add the minced beef and cook, stirring, until browned all over.

Stir in the tomatoes, kidney beans, stock, tomato purée (paste), sherry, chilli powder, herbs, cumin and salt and pepper and mix well. Bring slowly to the boil, cover and simmer gently for 45-60 minutes, stirring occasionally. Garnish with parsley sprigs and serve with freshly cooked rigatoni.

Serves 6. Makes 1 litre (35 fl oz/4½ cups).

Total Cals/Kj: 1192/4994   Total fat: 45.7 g
Cals/Kj per portion: 199/832   Fat per portion: 7.6 g
Cals/Kj per cup: 265/1110   Fat per cup: 10.1 g

— PEPPERONI & FRESH CHILLI —

1 teaspoon sunflower oil
300 g (10 oz) leeks, thinly sliced
1 red pepper (capsicum), sliced
1 fresh red chilli, seeded and sliced
1 fresh green chilli, seeded and sliced
1 clove garlic, crushed
575 g (1 ¼ lb) tomatoes, peeled, seeded and chopped
115 g (4 oz) pepperoni, thinly sliced
½ teaspoon ground coriander
salt and freshly ground black pepper
flat-leaf parsley, to garnish

In a large pan, heat the oil and cook the leeks, red pepper (capsicum), red and green chillies and garlic for 5 minutes.

Add the tomatoes, pepperoni, coriander and salt and pepper, mixing well.

Bring slowly to the boil, cover and simmer for 20-25 minutes, stirring occasionally. Garnish with parsley and serve with freshly cooked fusilli.

Serves 6. Makes 900 ml (32 fl oz/4 cups).

Total Cals/Kj: 835/3479   Total fat: 61.0 g
Cals/Kj per portion: 139/580   Fat per portion: 10.1 g
Cals/Kj per cup: 209/870   Fat per cup: 15.2 g

Note: In place of fresh chillies, use minced chilli, available in jars.

PARMA HAM & TOMATO

15 g (½ oz/1 tablespoon) half fat spread
4 shallots, finely chopped
1 tablespoon plain flour
300 ml (10 fl oz/1¼ cups) pork or vegetable stock
400 g (14 oz) can chopped tomatoes
225 g (8 oz) can chopped tomatoes
1 tablespoon chopped fresh thyme
few drops Worcestershire sauce
salt and freshly ground black pepper
115 g (4 oz) Parma ham, cut into thin strips
bay leaves and fresh thyme, to garnish

In a saucepan, melt the half fat spread over a low heat. Add the shallots and cook for 5 minutes, stirring occasionally.

Add the flour and cook for 1 minute, stirring. Remove the pan from the heat and gradually stir in the stock. Bring slowly to the boil, stirring, and continue to cook, stirring, until the mixture thickens. Add the tomatoes, thyme, Worcestershire sauce and salt and pepper and mix well. Return the mixture to the boil, cover and simmer for 15 minutes, stirring occasionally.

Uncover and simmer for 10 minutes to allow the sauce to thicken, stirring occasionally. Add the Parma ham and cook for 3 minutes. Garnish with bay leaves and thyme and serve with freshly cooked filled pasta such as tortellini or ravioli.

Serves 4. Makes 700 ml (24½ fl oz/3¼ cups).

Total Cals/Kj: 646/2705	Total fat: 39.7 g
Cals/Kj per portion: 162/676	Fat per portion: 9.9 g
Cals/Kj per cup: 199/832	Fat per cup: 12.2 g

CHINESE-STYLE PORK

4 tablespoons dry cider
4 tablespoons light soy sauce
2 tablespoons soft brown sugar
1 tablespoon Worcestershire sauce
1 tablespoon tomato purée (paste)
2 teaspoons mustard powder
1 clove garlic, crushed
450 g (1 lb) lean pork fillet, cut into thin strips
1 teaspoon sunflower oil
1 bunch spring onions, cut into 1 cm (½ in) lengths
175 g (6 oz) small broccoli flowerets
175 g (6 oz) button mushrooms, halved
1 tablespoon cornflour
salt and freshly ground black pepper
shredded spring onions, to garnish

In a bowl, mix together the cider, soy sauce, sugar, Worcestershire sauce, tomato purée (paste), mustard and garlic. Add the pork and stir until the meat is covered with the marinade. Cover, chill and leave to marinate for 1 hour. In a large frying pan or wok, heat the oil. Remove pork from the marinade with a slotted spoon, reserving the marinade, and add pork to the pan with spring onions, broccoli and mushrooms. Stir-fry over a high heat for 5-7 minutes, until the meat is browned and cooked. Blend cornflour with the marinade and 2 tablespoons water.

Add cornflour mixture to the pan with salt and pepper. Bring to the boil over a high heat, stirring continuously for 1-2 minutes, until the sauce is thickened and glossy. Garnish with spring onion and serve immediately with freshly cooked penne.

Serves 6. Makes 900 ml (32 fl oz/4 cups).

Total Cals/Kj: 1113/4671   Total fat: 43.1 g
Cals/Kj per portion: 186/779   Fat per portion: 7.2 g
Cals/Kj per cup: 278/1168   Fat per cup: 10.8 g

THAI-STYLE BEEF

1 tablespoon cornflour
150 ml (5 fl oz/⅔ cup) beef stock
70 ml (2½ fl oz/⅓ cup) red wine
1 tablespoon dark soy sauce
finely grated rind and juice of 1 lime
1 teaspoon each ground coriander and cumin
salt and freshly ground black pepper
2 teaspoons sesame oil
1 large onion, sliced
1 red pepper (capsicum), sliced
1 fresh green chilli, seeded and finely chopped
2.5 cm (1 in) piece fresh root ginger, peeled and
    finely chopped
2 cloves garlic, crushed
450 g (1 lb) lean fillet steak, cut into thin strips
1 tablespoon sesame seeds

In a bowl, mix together the cornflour, stock, wine, soy sauce, lime rind and juice, coriander, cumin and salt and pepper and set aside. In a large frying pan or wok, heat the oil and stir-fry the onion, pepper (capsicum), chilli, ginger and garlic for 1 minute. Add the steak and stir-fry for 3-5 minutes, until the meat is browned and cooked through.

Add the cornflour mixture and bring to the boil over a high heat, stirring continuously for 1-2 minutes, until the sauce is thickened and glossy. Sprinkle with sesame seeds, garnish with lemon wedges and coriander leaves and serve immediately with freshly cooked tagliatelle.

Serves 4. Makes 700 ml (24½ fl oz/3¼ cups).

Total Cals/Kj: 998/4186	Total fat: 42.6 g
Cals/Kj per portion: 250/1046	Fat per portion: 10.6 g
Cals/Kj per cup: 307/1288	Fat per cup: 13.1 g

GAMMON & PINEAPPLE

225 g (8 oz) can pineapple cubes in fruit juice
115 g (4 oz) sugar snap peas
175 g (6 oz) low fat soft cheese
150 ml (5 fl oz/ ⅔ cup) low fat plain yogurt
salt and freshly ground black pepper
350 g (12 oz) cooked lean gammon, chopped
4 sticks celery, thinly sliced
2 tablespoons chopped fresh parsley
chervil sprigs, to garnish

Drain the pineapple, reserving 3 tablespoons
of the juice. Finely chop half of the pineapple
cubes, halve the remainder and set aside.

Blanch the sugar snap peas in boiling water
for 30 seconds. Drain, rinse in cold water and
drain again. Set aside. Place the pineapple
juice, soft cheese, yogurt and salt and pepper
in a blender or food processor and blend
until smooth.

Place in a bowl and stir in the gammon,
pineapple, celery, sugar snap peas and parsley
and mix well. Garnish with chervil and serve
with freshly cooked conchiglie.

Serves 4. Makes 1.1 litres (38½ fl oz/5 cups).

Total Cals/Kj: 1051/4439   Total fat: 31.9 g
Cals/Kj per portion: 263/1100   Fat per portion: 8.0 g
Cals/Kj per cup: 210/888   Fat per cup: 6.4 g

BOLOGNESE

1 onion, chopped
1 clove garlic, crushed
450 g (1 lb) extra lean minced beef
3 carrots, finely chopped
175 g (6 oz) mushrooms, sliced
3 sticks celery, sliced
400 g (14 oz) can chopped tomatoes
1 tablespoon tomato purée (paste)
2 teaspoons dried mixed herbs
300 ml (10 fl oz/1¼ cups) beef stock
150 ml (5 fl oz/⅔ cup) dry white wine
salt and freshly ground black pepper
basil sprigs, to garnish

Place the onion and garlic in a large saucepan with the minced beef. Cook gently, stirring occasionally, until the mince is browned all over. Add the carrots, mushrooms and celery to the pan and cook for 5 minutes. Stir in the tomatoes, tomato purée (paste), mixed herbs, stock, wine and salt and pepper, mixing well. Bring slowly to the boil, cover and simmer for 1 hour, stirring occasionally.

Uncover, increase the heat slightly and simmer for 30 minutes, to thicken the sauce. Garnish with basil sprigs and serve with freshly cooked spaghetti.

Serves 6. Makes 1.2 litres (42 fl oz/5¼ cups).

Total Cals/Kj: 1046/4831   Total fat: 38.4 g
Cals/Kj per portion: 174/805   Fat per portion: 6.4 g
Cals/Kj per cup: 190/878   Fat per cup: 6.9 g

Variation: Use lean minced turkey or pork in place of the minced beef.

LIGHT CARBONARA

1 teaspoon olive oil
1 small onion, finely chopped
1 clove garlic, crushed
175 g (6 oz) lean cooked ham, cut into strips
3 eggs
85 g (3 oz/ ¾ cup) grated Parmesan cheese
4 tablespoons reduced fat single (light) cream
salt and freshly ground black pepper
parsley leaves, to garnish

In a saucepan, heat the oil and add the onion and garlic. Cook gently for 5 minutes. Add the ham and mix well.

In a bowl, mix together the eggs, grated Parmesan, cream and salt and pepper. Remove the saucepan from the heat and stir in the egg mixture.

Heat the mixture very gently, stirring continuously, until the eggs just begin to set. Serve immediately, mixed into freshly cooked tagliatelle or spaghetti and garnished with parsley.

Serves 6. Makes 500 ml (18 fl oz/2 ¼ cups).

Total Cals/Kj: 1084/4513   Total fat: 71.9 g
Cals/Kj per portion: 181/752   Fat per portion: 11.9 g
Cals/Kj per cup: 482/2006   Fat per cup: 31.9 g

BEEF & MUSTARD

4 shallots, sliced
1 clove garlic, crushed
150 ml (5 fl oz/⅔ cup) unsweetened red grape juice
4 tablespoons red wine vinegar
1 tablespoon lemon juice
2 tablespoons wholegrain mustard
1 tablespoon chopped fresh oregano
salt and freshly ground black pepper
450 g (1 lb) lean rump steak, cubed
2 teaspoons sunflower oil
2 tablespoons plain flour
150 ml (5 fl oz/⅔ cup) beef stock
fresh oregano, to garnish

In a bowl, mix together the shallots, garlic, grape juice, vinegar, lemon juice, mustard, oregano and salt and pepper and mix well. Add the steak and stir until the meat is coated with the marinade. Cover, chill and leave to marinate for 2-3 hours, stirring occasionally. In a large frying pan or wok, heat the oil. Remove the steak and shallots from the marinade with a slotted spoon, reserving the marinade, and add steak and shallots to the pan. Cook for 5 minutes, stirring, until the meat is browned. Add the flour and cook for 1 minute, stirring.

Remove the pan from the heat and gradually stir in the stock and marinade. Bring slowly to the boil, stirring, and continue to cook until the mixture thickens. Simmer gently for 8-10 minutes, until meat is tender, stirring occasionally. Garnish with oregano and serve with freshly cooked fusilli.

Serves 4. Makes 700 ml (24½ fl oz/3¼ cups).

Total Cals/Kj: 903/3798   Total fat: 35.0 g
Cals/Kj per portion: 226/950   Fat per portion: 8.8 g
Cals/Kj per cup: 278/1169   Fat per cup: 10.7 g

—— SPICY PORK MEATBALLS ——

450 g (1 lb) lean minced pork
1 onion, finely chopped
1 clove garlic, crushed
25 g (1 oz / ½ cup) fresh wholemeal breadcrumbs
2 tablespoons tomato purée (paste)
1 egg, beaten
1 teaspoon ground coriander
½ teaspoon each ground bay leaves, allspice and
   cayenne pepper
4 teaspoons seasoned plain flour
2 teaspoons olive oil
2 shallots, sliced
1 green and 1 red pepper (capsicum), chopped
400 g (14 oz) can chopped tomatoes
2 teaspoons dried mixed herbs
2 teaspoons Worcestershire sauce

In a bowl, mix together the pork, onion, garlic, breadcrumbs, 1 tablespoon tomato purée (paste), egg and spices until thoroughly combined. Form the mixture into walnut-sized balls and roll each ball in flour. Cover and chill for 1 hour. In a frying pan, heat 1 teaspoon of the oil and brown the meatballs all over, turning them carefully. In a large saucepan, heat the remaining oil and cook the shallots and peppers (capsicum) for 5 minutes.

Add the remaining 1 tablespoon tomato purée (paste), tomatoes, mixed herbs and Worcestershire sauce and mix well. Bring to the boil. Add the meatballs, stirring gently to cover them in sauce. Cover and simmer gently for 30 minutes, stirring occasionally. Serve with freshly cooked linguine.

Serves 6. Makes 1 litre (35 fl oz/4½ cups).

Total Cals/Kj: 1220/5122   Total fat: 54.1 g
Cals/Kj per portion: 203/854   Fat per portion: 9.0 g
Cals/Kj per cup: 271/1138   Fat per cup: 12.0 g

BEEF IN RED WINE

450 g (1 lb) lean stewing steak, cubed
2 tablespoons seasoned flour
25 g (1 oz/2 tablespoons) half fat spread
1 onion, chopped
55 g (2 oz) lean smoked streaky bacon, diced
2 carrots, sliced
115 g (4 oz) button mushrooms, halved
175 ml (6 fl oz/¾ cup) beef stock
175 ml (6 fl oz/¾ cup) red wine
2 teaspoons dried mixed herbs
salt and freshly ground black pepper
flat-leaf parsley and bay leaves, to garnish

Toss the beef in the flour. In a saucepan, melt
the half fat spread over a low heat.

Add the beef, onion and bacon and cook
gently for 8-10 minutes, until the meat is
browned all over. Add the carrots to the pan
with the mushrooms, stock, wine, mixed
herbs and salt and pepper, mixing well.

Bring slowly to the boil, cover and simmer
for 1½-2 hours, stirring occasionally.
Garnish with flat-leaf parsley and bay leaves
and serve with freshly cooked penne.

Serves 6. Makes 1.1 litres (38½ fl oz/5 cups).

Total Cals/Kj: 1227/5132   Total fat: 54.4 g
Cals/Kj per portion: 205/855   Fat per portion: 9.0 g
Cals/Kj per cup: 245/1026   Fat per cup: 10.9 g

—HAM, MUSHROOM & PEPPER—

2 teaspoons sunflower oil
1 small green pepper (capsicum), sliced
1 small red pepper (capsicum), sliced
1 clove garlic, crushed
300 g (10 oz) mushrooms, sliced
300 ml (10 fl oz/1 ¼ cups) pork or vegetable stock
225 g (8 oz) cooked lean ham, finely diced
2 teaspoons Dijon mustard
salt and freshly ground black pepper
1 tablespoon cornflour
3 tablespoons brandy
1-2 tablespoons chopped fresh basil
basil sprigs, to garnish

In a large frying pan or wok, heat the oil and cook the peppers (capsicums) and garlic for 5 minutes. Add the mushrooms and stock, cover and cook for 5 minutes, stirring occasionally. Stir in the ham, mustard and salt and pepper and cook for 3 minutes. In a bowl, blend the cornflour with the brandy and add to the pan.

Cook, stirring constantly, until the mixture has thickened, then simmer for 3 minutes. Stir in the basil. Garnish with basil sprigs and serve with freshly cooked farfalle.

Serves 4. Makes 900 ml (32 fl oz/4 cups).

Total Cals/Kj: 622/2598   Total fat: 24.7 g
Cals/Kj per portion: 155/649   Fat per portion: 6.1g
Cals/Kj per cup: 155/649   Fat per cup: 6.1 g

PEPPERED BEEF

450 g (1 lb) lean fillet steak, cut into thin strips
1 clove garlic, crushed
1 tablespoon black peppercorns, crushed
3 teaspoons olive oil
1 tablespoon cornflour
150 ml (5 fl oz/⅔ cup) beef stock
4 tablespoons dry white wine
2 tablespoons dark soy sauce
salt and freshly ground black pepper
1 red pepper (capsicum), sliced
1 bunch spring onions, cut into 1 cm (½ in) lengths
2 courgettes (zucchini), cut into matchstick strips
fresh coriander, to garnish

In a bowl, mix together the steak, garlic, peppercorns and 2 teaspoons oil. Cover and chill for 3-4 hours, stirring occasionally. In another bowl, blend the cornflour with the stock, wine, soy sauce and salt and pepper and set aside. In a large frying pan or wok, heat the remaining 1 teaspoon oil and cook the pepper (capsicum), spring onions and courgettes (zucchini) over a high heat for 3 minutes, stirring. Add the steak mixture and cook for 3 minutes, stirring, until the meat is cooked through.

Add the cornflour mixture to the pan and cook, stirring continuously, until the mixture thickens. Simmer gently for 3 minutes. Garnish with coriander and serve with freshly cooked rigatoni.

Serves 6. Makes 900 ml (32 fl oz/4 cups).

Total Cals/Kj: 942/3942   Total fat: 38.4 g
Cals/Kj per portion: 157/657   Fat per portion: 6.4 g
Cals/Kj per cup: 236/986   Fat per cup: 9.6 g

— CREAMED CELERY & HAM —

1 small onion, sliced
1 small carrot, sliced
1 bay leaf
6 black peppercorns
300 ml (10 fl oz/1 ¼ cups) semi-skimmed milk
25 g (1 oz/2 tablespoons) half fat spread
1 onion, finely chopped
4 sticks celery, finely chopped
25 g (1 oz/ ¼ cup) plain flour
225 g (8 oz) cooked lean ham, finely chopped
1 tablespoon chopped fresh thyme
salt and freshly ground black pepper
2 tablespoons reduced fat single (light) cream
fresh thyme, to garnish

Place the onion, carrot, bay leaf and peppercorns in a saucepan with the milk and bring slowly to the boil. Remove the pan from the heat, cover and set aside to infuse for 20 minutes. Strain into a bowl and discard the vegetables. In a saucepan, melt the half fat spread over a low heat. Add the chopped onion and celery, cover and cook gently for 10 minutes, stirring occasionally. Stir in the flour and cook for 1 minute, stirring. Remove the pan from the heat and gradually stir in the flavoured milk.

Bring slowly to the boil, stirring, and continue to cook, stirring, until the mixture thickens. Add the ham, thyme and salt and pepper and simmer gently for 5 minutes. Remove the pan from the heat and stir in the cream. Garnish with thyme and serve with freshly cooked filled pasta such as ravioli.

Serves 4. Makes 800 ml (28 fl oz/3 ½ cups).

Total Cals/Kj: 711/2988   Total fat: 30.8 g
Cals/Kj per portion: 178/747   Fat per portion: 7.7 g
Cals/Kj per cup: 203/854   Fat per cup: 8.8 g

MEXICAN PORK

450 g (1 lb) lean pork fillet, cubed
2 tablespoons seasoned flour
25 g (1 oz/2 tablespoons) half fat spread
2 onions, sliced
2 cloves garlic, crushed
300 ml (10 fl oz/1 ¼ cups) tomato juice
400 g (14 oz) can chopped tomatoes
400 g (14 oz) can red kidney beans, rinsed and
    drained
1 teaspoon ground cumin
½ teaspoon ground coriander
½ teaspoon hot chilli powder
½ teaspoon each dried basil and oregano
salt and freshly ground black pepper
3 courgettes (zucchini), sliced
basil sprigs, to garnish

Toss the pork fillet in the seasoned flour. In a
large saucepan, melt the half fat spread over a
low heat. Cook the onions and garlic for
3 minutes. Add the pork and cook gently for
3-5 minutes, stirring occasionally, until the
meat is browned all over. Stir in the tomato
juice, tomatoes, kidney beans, spices, herbs
and salt and pepper and mix well. Bring
slowly to the boil, cover and simmer gently
for 1-1½ hours, until the meat is tender,
stirring occasionally.

Add the courgettes (zucchini) 10 minutes
before the end of cooking time. Garnish with
basil sprigs and serve with freshly cooked
tagliatelle or tagliarini.

Serves 6. Makes 1.3 litres (45½ fl oz/5¾ cups).

Total Cals/Kj: 1404/5902   Total fat: 49.4 g
Cals/Kj per portion: 234/984   Fat per portion: 8.2 g
Cals/Kj per cup: 244/1026   Fat per cup: 8.6 g

Note: For authentic flavours and aromas, use
a pestle and mortar to crush your own spices.

— SHREDDED BEEF & GINGER —

1 tablespoon cornflour
175 ml (6 fl oz/ ¾ cup) beef stock
70 ml (2 ½ fl oz/ ⅓ cup) dry sherry
2 teaspoons caster sugar
salt and freshly ground black pepper
2 teaspoons olive oil
2 carrots, cut into matchstick strips
5 cm (2 in) piece fresh root ginger, peeled and finely
    chopped
2 cloves garlic, crushed
350 g (12 oz) lean rump steak, cut into thin strips
175 g (6 oz) mange tout (snow peas)

In a bowl, blend the cornflour with the stock, sherry, sugar and salt and pepper and set aside. In a large frying pan or wok, heat the oil over a high heat and stir-fry the carrots, ginger and garlic for 2 minutes. Add the steak and stir-fry for 3 minutes, until the meat is browned all over and cooked through. Add the mange tout (snow peas) and stir-fry for 1 minute.

Add the cornflour mixture and bring to the boil over a high heat, stirring continuously for 1-2 minutes, until the sauce is thickened and glossy. Serve immediately with freshly cooked fusilli.

Serves 4. Makes 800 ml (28 fl oz/3 ½ cups).

Total Cals/Kj: 850/3565   Total fat: 27.3 g
Cals/Kj per portion: 213/891   Fat per portion: 6.8 g
Cals/Kj per cup: 243/1018   Fat per cup: 7.8 g

Variation: Use ginger wine instead of sherry.

— SPICY SAUSAGE & TOMATO —

450 g (1 lb) low fat sausages
1 teaspoon sunflower oil
1 onion, sliced
1 clove garlic, crushed
1 fresh green chilli, seeded and finely chopped
2 teaspoons dried thyme
2 teaspoons garam masala
1 teaspoon turmeric
½ teaspoon chilli powder
175 g (6 oz) mushrooms, sliced
150 ml (5 fl oz/⅔ cup) pork or vegetable stock
400 g (14 oz) can chopped tomatoes
salt and freshly ground black pepper
fresh thyme and parsley, to garnish

Heat a frying pan and cook the sausages for 8-10 minutes until browned all over. Cut into 2.5 cm (1 in) pieces. In a saucepan, heat the oil and cook the onion, garlic and chilli for 5 minutes. Add the thyme and spices and cook, stirring, for 1 minute.

Add the sausages, mushrooms, stock, tomatoes and salt and pepper. Mix gently but thoroughly and bring the mixture to the boil. Cover and simmer for 20 minutes, stirring occasionally, until the sausages are cooked through. Garnish with thyme and parsley and serve with freshly cooked penne.

Serves 6. Makes 1.2 litres (42 fl oz/5 ¼ cups).

Total Cals/Kj: 1026/4296   Total fat: 52.9 g
Cals/Kj per portion: 171/716   Fat per portion: 8.8 g
Cals/Kj per cup: 195/818   Fat per cup: 10.0 g

—— BEEF & MANGE TOUT ——

1 tablespoon cornflour
150 ml (5 fl oz/⅔ cup) beef stock
70 ml (2½ fl oz/⅓ cup) tomato juice
1 tablespoon tomato purée (paste)
2 tablespoons dark soy sauce
2 teaspoons Worcestershire sauce
1 tablespoon soft brown sugar
salt and freshly ground black pepper
2 teaspoons walnut oil
2 cloves garlic, crushed
1 bunch spring onions, cut into 1 cm (½ in) lengths
4 sticks celery, thinly sliced
5 cm (2 in) piece fresh root ginger, peeled and finely
   chopped
450 g (1 lb) rump steak, cubed
225 g (8 oz) mange tout (snow peas)

In a bowl, blend the cornflour with the stock, tomato juice, tomato purée (paste), soy sauce, Worcestershire sauce, sugar and salt and pepper. Set aside. In a large frying pan or wok, heat the oil and add the garlic, spring onions, celery and ginger and stir-fry over a high heat for 1 minute. Add the beef and stir-fry for 3-5 minutes, until the meat is browned. Add the mange tout (snow peas) and cook for 1 minute.

Add the cornflour mixture to the pan and bring to the boil over a high heat, stirring continuously for 1-2 minutes, until the sauce is thickened and glossy. Serve immediately with freshly cooked fettucine or tagliatelle.

Serves 6. Makes 1 litre (35 fl oz/4½ cups).

Total Cals/Kj: 934/3938   Total fat: 32.8 g
Cals/Kj per portion: 156/656   Fat per portion: 5.5 g
Cals/Kj per cup: 208/875   Fat per cup: 7.3 g

— SMOKED HAM & TOMATO —

700 g (1½ lb) tomatoes, peeled, seeded and chopped
225 g (8 oz) leeks, sliced
2 carrots, finely diced
2 sticks celery, thinly sliced
1 clove garlic, crushed
1 tablespoon tomato purée (paste)
2 teaspoons caster sugar
few drops Tabasco sauce
salt and freshly ground black pepper
175 g (6 oz) lean cooked smoked ham, diced
1-2 tablespoons chopped fresh basil
2 tablespoons reduced fat single (light) cream
basil sprigs, to garnish

Place the tomatoes, leeks, carrots, celery, garlic, tomato purée (paste), sugar, Tabasco and salt and pepper in a saucepan and mix well. Bring gently to the boil, cover and simmer for 10 minutes, stirring occasionally. Stir in the ham and cook for a further 10 minutes, stirring occasionally.

Remove the pan from the heat and stir in the basil and cream. Garnish with basil sprigs and serve with freshly cooked pipe rigate or conchiglie.

Serves 4. Makes 1 litre (35 fl oz/4½ cups).

Total Cals/Kj: 545/2300   Total fat: 15.9 g
Cals/Kj per portion: 136/575   Fat per portion: 3.9 g
Cals/Kj per cup: 121/511   Fat per cup: 3.5 g

Note: If the tomato mixture is too dry, add 55 ml (2 fl oz/¼ cup) water with the ham.

— PARMA HAM & ASPARAGUS —

350 g (12 oz) asparagus
2 teaspoons walnut oil
1 onion, finely chopped
1 clove garlic, crushed
115 g (4 oz) Parma ham, cut into thin strips
1 tablespoon cornflour
175 ml (6 fl oz/¾ cup) vegetable stock
70 ml (2½ fl oz/⅓ cup) dry white wine
1 tablespoon light soy sauce
2 teaspoons Dijon mustard
salt and freshly ground black pepper
rosemary sprigs, to garnish

Trim the woody ends from the asparagus and cut the stems into 1 cm (½ in) lengths.

In a saucepan, heat the oil over a high heat and cook the asparagus, onion and garlic for 5 minutes. Reduce the heat, add the ham and cook for 1 minute. In a bowl, blend the cornflour, stock, wine, soy sauce, mustard and salt and pepper and add to the pan.

Bring to the boil, stirring, and continue to cook, stirring, until the mixture thickens. Simmer for 5 minutes. Garnish with rosemary sprigs and serve with freshly cooked linguine.

Serves 3. Makes 550 ml (20 fl oz/2½ cups).

Total Cals/Kj: 721/2987   Total fat: 45.4 g
Cals/Kj per portion: 240/996   Fat per portion: 15.1 g
Cals/Kj per cup: 288/1195   Fat per cup: 18.1 g

— COUNTRY-STYLE CHICKEN —

2 teaspoons olive oil
1 onion, sliced
2 cloves garlic, crushed
1 green pepper (capsicum), sliced
2 carrots, sliced
450 g (1 lb) skinless, boneless chicken breasts, cut
    into thin strips
55 g (2 oz) lean smoked streaky bacon, diced
175 g (6 oz) button mushrooms
450 ml (16 fl oz/2 cups) chicken stock
3 tablespoons tomato purée (paste)
1 teaspoon dried mixed herbs
salt and freshly ground black pepper
1 tablespoon cornflour
marjoram sprigs, to garnish

In a large frying pan or wok, heat the oil, add the onion, garlic, pepper (capsicum) and carrots and cook for 5 minutes. Add the chicken and bacon and cook until the chicken is lightly browned all over, stirring occasionally. Stir in the mushrooms, stock, tomato purée (paste), mixed herbs and salt and pepper, mixing well. Bring slowly to the boil, cover and simmer gently for 15 minutes, until the chicken is cooked and tender, stirring occasionally.

In a small bowl, blend the cornflour with 2 tablespoons water and add to the pan. Bring back to the boil and continue to cook, stirring continuously, until the mixture thickens. Simmer for 2-3 minutes. Garnish with marjoram sprigs and serve with freshly cooked lasagnette or tagliatelle.

Serves 6. Makes 1.3 litres (45½ fl oz/5¾ cups).

Total Cals/Kj: 1040/4356   Total fat: 48.4 g
Cals/Kj per portion: 173/726   Fat per portion: 8.0 g
Cals/Kj per cup: 181/757   Fat per cup: 8.4 g

──CHICKEN IN WHITE WINE──

25 g (1 oz/2 tablespoons) half fat spread
1 shallot, thinly sliced
225 g (8 oz) mushrooms, sliced
25 g (1 oz/¼ cup) plain flour
115 ml (4 fl oz/½ cup) chicken stock
175 ml (6 fl oz/¾ cup) dry white wine
450 g (1 lb) cooked chicken, cubed
115 g (4 oz) seedless grapes, halved
salt and freshly ground black pepper
2 tablespoons reduced fat single (light) cream
1 tablespoon chopped fresh tarragon
tarragon sprigs, to garnish

In a saucepan, melt the half fat spread over a low heat and cook the shallot and mushrooms for 5 minutes.

Add the flour and cook for 1 minute, stirring. Gradually stir in the stock and wine. Bring slowly to the boil, stirring, and continue to cook until the mixture thickens.

Add the chicken to the sauce with the grapes and salt and pepper and simmer gently for 5 minutes, stirring. Remove the pan from the heat and stir in the cream and tarragon. Garnish with tarragon sprigs and serve with freshly cooked spaghettini or tagliarini.

Serves 6. Makes 950 ml (33 fl oz/4¼ cups).

Total Cals/Kj: 1168/4911
Cals/Kj per portion: 195/819
Cals/Kj per cup: 275/1155

Total fat: 36.7 g
Fat per portion: 6.1 g
Fat per cup: 8.6 g

CHICKEN ITALIENNE

450 g (1 lb) skinless, boneless chicken breasts, cubed
2 tablespoons seasoned plain flour
2 teaspoons olive oil
350 g (12 oz) button onions, halved
1 clove garlic, crushed
250 ml (9 fl oz/1 cup) chicken stock
175 ml (6 fl oz/¾ cup) dry white wine
225 g (8 oz) can chopped tomatoes
1 tablespoon tomato purée (paste)
1 tablespoon chopped fresh mixed herbs
salt and freshly ground black pepper
flat-leaf parsley, to garnish

Toss the chicken in the seasoned flour.

In a large saucepan, heat the oil and cook the onions and garlic for 5 minutes. Add the chicken and cook until lightly browned all over. Gradually stir in the stock and wine, then add the tomatoes, tomato purée (paste), herbs and salt and pepper, mixing well.

Bring slowly to the boil, cover and simmer for 25 minutes, stirring occasionally, until the chicken is cooked and tender. Garnish with flat-leaf parsley and serve with freshly cooked linguine or fettucine.

Serves 6. Makes 1.2 litres (42 fl oz/5¼ cups).

Total Cals/Kj: 1026/4312   Total fat: 25.7 g
Cals/Kj per portion: 171/719   Fat per portion: 4.3 g
Cals/Kj per cup: 195/821   Fat per cup: 4.9 g

—— PIQUANT CHICKEN & HAM ——

45 g (1½ oz/3 tablespoons) half fat spread
45 g (1½ oz/⅓ cup) plain flour
450 ml (16 fl oz/2 cups) semi-skimmed milk
2 teaspoons tandoori powder
1 teaspoon garam masala
225 g (8 oz) cooked chicken, diced
225 g (8 oz) lean cooked ham, cut into strips
salt and freshly ground black pepper
2 tablespoons chopped fresh parsley
fresh coriander, to garnish

In a large saucepan, melt the half fat spread over a low heat. Add the flour and cook for 1 minute, stirring.

Remove the pan from the heat and gradually stir in the milk. Bring slowly to the boil, stirring, and continue to cook, stirring, until the mixture thickens.

Add the spices, chicken, ham and salt and pepper and simmer gently for 5 minutes, stirring. Stir in the parsley. Garnish with fresh coriander and serve with freshly cooked conchiglie.

Serves 6. Makes 800 ml (28 fl oz/3½ cups).

Total Cals/Kj: 1212/5092   Total fat: 50.5 g
Cals/Kj per portion: 202/849   Fat per portion: 8.4 g
Cals/Kj per cup: 346/1455   Fat per cup: 14.4 g

-MARINATED TURKEY & MINT-

115 ml (4 fl oz/ ½ cup) dry white wine
2 tablespoons light soy sauce
1 tablespoon lemon juice
1 clove garlic, crushed
4 tablespoons chopped fresh mint
450 g (1 lb) skinless turkey escalopes, cut into thin
    strips
2 teaspoons sunflower oil
1 onion, sliced
4 carrots, cut into matchstick strips
3 courgettes (zucchini), thinly sliced
1 tablespoon cornflour
300 ml (10 fl oz/1 ¼ cups) chicken stock
salt and freshly ground black pepper
mint sprigs, to garnish

In a bowl, mix together the wine, soy sauce, lemon juice, garlic and 2 tablespoons mint. Add the turkey and mix well. Cover, chill and leave to marinate for 2-3 hours. In a large frying pan or wok, heat the oil over a high heat and stir-fry the onion, carrots and courgettes (zucchini) for 2 minutes. Remove the turkey from the marinade with a slotted spoon, reserving the marinade, and add the turkey to the pan. Stir-fry over a high heat for 3-4 minutes, until the turkey is cooked.

In a bowl, blend the cornflour with the marinade and stock and add to pan with the salt and pepper. Bring to the boil over a high heat, stirring for 1-2 minutes, until the sauce is thickened and glossy. Add the remaining mint. Garnish with mint sprigs and serve immediately with freshly cooked spaghetti.

Serves 6. Makes 1.2 litres (42 fl oz/5 ¼ cups).

Total Cals/Kj: 964/4038   Total fat: 18.3 g
Cals/Kj per portion: 161/673   Fat per portion: 3.0 g
Cals/Kj per cup: 184/770   Fat per cup: 3.5 g

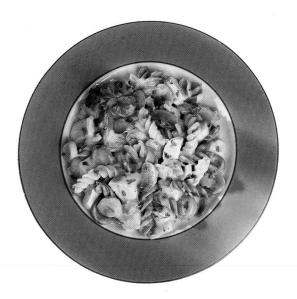

— CHICKEN & MUSHROOM —

45 g (1½ oz/3 tablespoons) half fat spread
2 leeks, thinly sliced
225 g (8 oz) mushrooms, sliced
45 g (1½ oz/⅓ cup) plain flour
300 ml (10 fl oz/1¼ cups) semi-skimmed milk
150 ml (5 fl oz/⅔ cup) chicken stock
350 g (12 oz) cooked chicken, cut into small pieces
salt and freshly ground black pepper
1 tablespoon chopped fresh parsley
parsley sprigs, to garnish

In a saucepan, melt the half fat spread over a low heat. Add the leeks and mushrooms, cover and cook gently for 8 minutes until soft, stirring occasionally.

Add the flour and cook for 1 minute, stirring. Remove the pan from the heat and gradually stir in the milk and stock. Bring slowly to the boil, stirring, and continue to cook, stirring, until the mixture thickens.

Add the chicken and salt and pepper and simmer gently for 5 minutes, stirring. Stir in the parsley. Garnish with parsley sprigs and serve with freshly cooked fusilli.

Serves 6. Makes 1.2 litres (42 fl oz/5¼ cups).

Total Cals/Kj: 1139/4792   Total fat: 43.7 g
Cals/Kj per portion: 190/798   Fat per portion: 7.3 g
Cals/Kj per cup: 217/913   Fat per cup: 8.3 g

Variation: Use chopped fresh tarragon or coriander in place of the parsley.

—— SWEET & SOUR CHICKEN ——

2 tablespoons each light soy sauce and dry sherry
450 g (1 lb) skinless, boneless chicken breasts, cut
　　into thin strips
2 teaspoons walnut oil
1 red pepper (capsicum), sliced
1 bunch spring onions, cut into 1 cm (½ in) lengths
3 carrots, thinly sliced
3 sticks celery, thinly sliced
1 clove garlic, crushed
2 tablespoons cornflour
150 ml (5 fl oz/⅔ cup) chicken stock
150 ml (5 fl oz/⅔ cup) unsweetened apple juice
2 tablespoons white wine vinegar
2 tablespoons tomato purée (paste)
3 tablespoons clear honey
spring onion strips, to garnish

In a bowl, mix together the soy sauce, sherry and chicken. Cover and leave to marinate for 30 minutes. In a large frying pan or wok, heat the oil over a high heat and stir-fry the pepper (capsicum), spring onions, carrots, celery and garlic for 3 minutes. Remove the chicken from the marinade using a slotted spoon, reserving the marinade, and add the chicken to the pan. Stir-fry over a high heat for 5 minutes, until the chicken is cooked.

In a jug, blend the cornflour with the marinade, stock, apple juice, vinegar, tomato purée (paste) and honey and add to the pan. Bring to the boil, stirring, until the sauce has thickened. Simmer for 3 minutes, stirring. Garnish with spring onion strips and serve with freshly cooked tagliatelle or spaghetti.

Serves 6. Makes 1.2 litres (42 fl oz/5¼ cups).

Total Cals/Kj: 1144/4826　　Total fat: 27.5 g
Cals/Kj per portion: 191/804　Fat per portion: 4.6 g
Cals/Kj per cup: 218/919　　Fat per cup: 5.2 g

── CHICKEN & SWEETCORN ──

115 g (4 oz) frozen peas or petits pois
250 ml (9 fl oz/1 cup) very low fat plain fromage frais
4 tablespoons Greek yogurt
4 tablespoons reduced calorie mayonnaise
200 g (7 oz) can sweetcorn kernels, drained
8 spring onions, thinly sliced
350 g (12 oz) cooked chicken, cubed
1 tablespoon chopped fresh coriander
salt and freshly ground black pepper
chopped fresh chives, to garnish

In a pan of boiling water, cook the peas for 3-5 minutes. Drain and set aside to cool. In a bowl, mix together the fromage frais, yogurt and mayonnaise.

Add the cooled peas, sweetcorn, spring onions, chicken, coriander and salt and pepper and mix gently but thoroughly. Garnish with chives and serve with freshly cooked farfalle.

Serves 6. Makes 900 ml (32 fl oz/4 cups).

Total Cals/Kj: 1300/5475	Total fat: 44.9 g
Cals/Kj per portion: 217/913	Fat per portion: 7.5 g
Cals/Kj per cup: 325/1369	Fat per cup: 11.2 g

Variation: Use other meats or fish such as ham, turkey or tuna, in place of the chicken.

– LEMON CHICKEN WITH BASIL –

finely grated rind of 1 lemon
juice of 2 lemons
2 cloves garlic, crushed
3 teaspoons olive oil
4 tablespoons chopped fresh basil
salt and freshly ground black pepper
450 g (1 lb) skinless, boneless chicken breasts, cubed
1 onion, sliced
3 sticks celery, thinly sliced
175 g (6 oz) button mushrooms, halved
2 tablespoons plain flour
150 ml (5 fl oz/ ⅔ cup) chicken stock
150 ml (5 fl oz/ ⅔ cup) dry white wine
lemon rind, lemon twists and basil sprigs, to garnish

In a bowl, mix together the lemon rind, lemon juice, garlic, 2 teaspoons of the oil, 2 tablespoons basil and salt and pepper. Add the chicken and mix well. Cover and chill for 1 hour. Heat remaining 1 teaspoon oil in a large frying pan or wok and cook the onion for 3 minutes. Remove the chicken from the marinade with a slotted spoon, reserving the marinade, and add chicken to the pan. Cook until chicken is lightly browned. Add celery and mushrooms and cook for 2 minutes.

Add the flour and cook for 1 minute, stirring. Remove pan from heat and gradually add the stock, wine and marinade. Bring to the boil and cook, stirring, until the mixture thickens. Cover and simmer gently for 15 minutes, stirring occasionally. Stir in remaining basil. Garnish and serve with freshly cooked linguine.

Serves 4. Makes 900 ml (32 fl oz/4 cups).

Total Cals/Kj: 972/4088
Cals/Kj per portion: 243/1022
Cals/Kj per cup: 243/1022

Total fat: 31.5 g
Fat per portion: 7.9 g
Fat per cup: 7.9 g

─── CHICKEN & MANGO ───

2 teaspoons olive oil
1 onion, chopped
2 cloves garlic, crushed
350 g (12 oz) skinless, boneless chicken breasts,
    cubed
3 tablespoons plain flour
350 ml (12 fl oz/1 ½ cups) chicken stock
250 ml (9 fl oz/1 cup) dry white wine
salt and freshly ground black pepper
55 g (2 oz/⅓ cup) raisins
1 ripe mango
2 tablespoons chopped fresh parsley

In a large saucepan, heat the oil and cook the
onion and garlic for 3 minutes.

Add the chicken and cook until lightly
browned all over. Sprinkle over the flour and
cook for 1 minute, stirring. Remove the pan
from the heat and gradually stir in the stock
and wine. Add the salt and pepper and bring
slowly to the boil, stirring continuously.
Cover and simmer for 30 minutes, stirring
occasionally. Stir in the raisins and cook for
a further 10 minutes.

Peel and stone the mango and purée the flesh
in a blender or food processor until smooth.
Add the mango purée and parsley to the pan
and cook gently for 5 minutes, until the
sauce is warmed through. Serve with freshly
cooked penne.

Serves 6. Makes 1 litre (35 fl oz/4 ½ cups).

Total Cals/Kj: 1152/4856   Total fat: 22.7 g
Cals/Kj per portion: 192/809   Fat per portion: 3.4 g
Cals/Kj per cup: 256/1079   Fat per cup: 5.0 g

CHICKEN TIKKA

150 ml (5 fl oz / ⅔ cup) tomato juice
1 onion, chopped
1 clove garlic, crushed
2.5 cm (1 in) piece fresh root ginger, peeled and
    chopped
1 fresh green chilli, seeded and chopped
juice of 1 lemon
2 teaspoons olive oil
2 teaspoons paprika
1 teaspoon each garam masala and ground cumin
salt and freshly ground black pepper
450 g (1 lb) skinless, boneless chicken breasts, cubed
150 ml (5 fl oz / ⅔ cup) reduced fat single (light)
    cream
1-2 tablespoons chopped fresh coriander
fresh coriander, to garnish

Place the tomato juice, onion, garlic, ginger, chilli, lemon juice, oil, spices and salt and pepper in a blender or food processor and blend until smooth. Pour into a bowl, add the chicken and stir until well coated. Cover and chill overnight to marinate. Preheat oven to 200C (400F/Gas 6). Place the chicken and sauce in a roasting tin and cook in the oven for 30 minutes, stirring occasionally.

Remove from the oven and stir in the cream and coriander. Return to the oven and cook for a further 10 minutes, until the sauce has warmed through. Garnish with coriander and serve with freshly cooked rigatoni.

Serves 6. Makes 800 ml (28 fl oz/3 ½ cups).

Total Cals/Kj: 986/4141   Total fat: 42.2 g
Cals/Kj per portion: 164/690   Fat per portion: 7.0 g
Cals/Kj per cup: 282/1183   Fat per cup: 12.0 g

SMOKED TURKEY

175 ml (6 fl oz/ ¾ cup) low fat plain yogurt
4 tablespoons reduced calorie mayonnaise
4 tablespoons Greek yogurt
225 g (8 oz) cooked, smoked lean turkey
175 g (6 oz) radishes
115 g (4 oz) sugar snap peas
2 tablespoons chopped fresh tarragon
salt and freshly ground black pepper
tarragon sprigs, to garnish

In a bowl, mix together the plain yogurt, mayonnaise and Greek yogurt.

Cut the turkey into thin strips. Top and tail the radishes and sugar snap peas and slice. Add to the yogurt mixture with the turkey and mix well.

Add the chopped tarragon and salt and pepper and mix well. Garnish with tarragon sprigs and serve with freshly cooked tagliatelle or spaghettini.

Serves 4. Makes 850 ml (30 fl oz/3¾ cups).

Total Cals/Kj: 725/3035	Total fat: 30.1 g
Cals/Kj per portion: 181/759	Fat per portion: 7.5 g
Cals/Kj per cup: 193/809	Fat per cup: 8.0 g

Variation: Use smoked chicken in place of the turkey and coriander or mint in place of the tarragon.

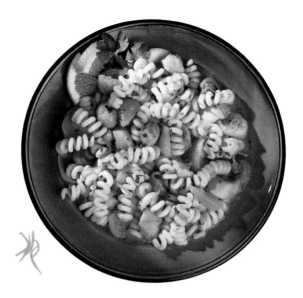

——— CHICKEN A L'ORANGE ———

25 g (1 oz/2 tablespoons) half fat spread
450 g (1 lb) button onions, halved
450 g (1 lb) skinless, boneless chicken breasts, cubed
2 tablespoons plain flour
225 g (8 oz) button mushrooms
grated rind of 1 large orange
juice of 3 large oranges
150 ml (5 fl oz/⅔ cup) dry cider
1 tablespoon soft brown sugar
salt and freshly ground black pepper
2 tablespoons chopped fresh parsley
orange slices and flat-leaf parsley, to garnish

In a large saucepan, melt the half fat spread and cook the onions for 5 minutes.

Add the chicken and cook gently until lightly browned all over. Sprinkle over the flour and cook for 1 minute, stirring. Add the mushrooms and orange rind, then gradually stir in the orange juice, cider, sugar and salt and pepper, mixing well.

Bring slowly to the boil, stirring, then cover and simmer for 20 minutes, stirring occasionally. Stir in the parsley. Garnish with orange slices and flat-leaf parsley and serve with freshly cooked fusilli.

Serves 6. Makes 1.2 litres (42 fl oz/5 ¼ cups).

Total Cals/Kj: 1046/4402   Total fat: 27.0 g
Cals/Kj per portion: 174/734   Fat per portion: 4.5 g
Cals/Kj per cup: 199/838   Fat per cup: 5.1 g

—— CHICKEN & BROCCOLI ——

175 g (6 oz) small broccoli flowerets
25 g (1 oz/2 tablespoons) half fat spread
1 small onion, finely chopped
2 courgettes (zucchini), sliced
115 g (4 oz) mushrooms, sliced
25 g (1 oz/¼ cup) plain flour
150 ml (5 fl oz/⅔ cup) semi-skimmed milk
175 ml (6 fl oz/¾ cup) chicken stock
350 g (12 oz) cooked chicken, cubed
salt and freshly ground black pepper
1 tablespoon chopped fresh oregano

Steam the broccoli over a pan of boiling
water for 4-5 minutes until tender. Set aside.

In a large saucepan, melt the half fat spread
over a low heat. Add the onion, courgettes
(zucchini) and mushrooms, cover and cook
for 10 minutes, stirring occasionally. Stir in
the flour and cook for 1 minute, stirring.
Remove the pan from the heat and gradually
stir in the milk and stock. Bring slowly to the
boil, stirring, and continue to cook, stirring,
until the mixture thickens.

Add the broccoli, chicken, salt and pepper
and oregano and simmer for 5 minutes,
stirring occasionally. Serve with freshly
cooked tagliatelle or spaghetti.

Serves 6. Makes 1.1 litres (38½ fl oz/5 cups).

Total Cals/Kj: 984/4130   Total fat: 33.6 g
Cals/Kj per portion: 164/688   Fat per portion: 5.6 g
Cals/Kj per cup: 197/826   Fat per cup: 6.7 g

—— TURKEY & GINGER ——

2 teaspoons sunflower oil
1 onion, sliced
3 carrots, thinly sliced
2 sticks celery, thinly sliced
2 courgettes (zucchini), thinly sliced
5 cm (2 in) piece fresh root ginger, peeled and finely
   chopped
350 g (12 oz) skinless turkey breasts, cut into strips
1 tablespoon cornflour
150 ml (5 fl oz/⅔ cup) ginger wine
115 ml (4 fl oz/½ cup) chicken stock
4 tablespoons unsweetened orange juice
salt and freshly ground black pepper
flat-leaf parsley, to garnish

In a large frying pan or wok, heat the oil over a high heat. Add the onion, carrots, celery, courgettes (zucchini), ginger and turkey and stir-fry for 5-7 minutes, until the turkey is cooked through. In a small bowl, blend the cornflour with the ginger wine, stock and orange juice and add to the pan with the salt and pepper.

Bring to the boil and cook over a high heat, stirring continuously, for 1-2 minutes, until the sauce is thickened and glossy. Garnish with flat-leaf parsley and serve with freshly cooked linguine.

Serves 6. Makes 1.1 litres (38½ fl oz/5 cups).

Total Cals/Kj: 967/4057   Total fat: 16.7 g
Cals/Kj per portion: 161/676   Fat per portion: 2.8 g
Cals/Kj per cup: 193/811   Fat per cup: 3.3 g

SPICY PRAWNS

2 teaspoons sunflower oil
1 bunch spring onions, cut into 1 cm (½ in) lengths
2 cloves garlic, crushed
1 small fresh red chilli, seeded and finely chopped
175 g (6 oz) button mushrooms, halved
1 teaspoon ground coriander
1 teaspoon ground cumin
1 teaspoon ground turmeric
½ teaspoon ground ginger
150 ml (5 fl oz/⅔ cup) fish stock
70 ml (2½ fl oz/⅓ cup) dry sherry
salt and freshly ground black pepper
450 g (1 lb) cooked, peeled prawns
1 tablespoon cornflour
fresh coriander, to garnish

In a saucepan, heat the oil and cook the spring onions, garlic and chilli for 2 minutes. Add the mushrooms and spices and cook, stirring, for 1 minute. Stir in the stock, sherry and salt and pepper. Bring to the boil, cover and simmer for 5 minutes, stirring occasionally. Add the prawns and cook gently for 1 minute.

In a small bowl, blend the cornflour with 2 tablespoons water and add to the pan. Bring back to the boil, stirring continuously, until the mixture thickens. Simmer gently for 3 minutes. Garnish with coriander and serve with freshly cooked spaghetti or tagliarini.

Serves 4. Makes 850 ml (30 fl oz/3¾ cups).

Total Cals/Kj: 795/3340   Total fat: 22.6 g
Cals/Kj per portion: 199/835   Fat per portion: 5.6 g
Cals/Kj per cup: 212/891   Fat per cup: 6.0 g

──── SALMON & COURGETTE ────

25 g (1 oz/2 tablespoons) half fat spread
2 courgettes (zucchini), cut into matchstick strips
2 shallots, finely chopped
25 g (1 oz/ ¼ cup) plain flour
300 ml (10 fl oz/1 ¼ cups) semi-skimmed milk
215 g (7 ½ oz) can red salmon, drained and flaked
dash of Tabasco sauce
1 tablespoon chopped fresh chives
salt and freshly ground black pepper
lemon slices and chives, to garnish

In a saucepan, melt the half fat spread over a low heat. Add the courgettes (zucchini) and shallots and cook gently for 8 minutes, stirring occasionally.

Stir in the flour and cook for 1 minute, stirring. Remove the pan from the heat and gradually stir in the milk. Bring slowly to the boil, stirring, and continue to cook, stirring, until the mixture thickens.

Add the salmon, Tabasco, chives and salt and pepper and simmer gently for 5 minutes, stirring. Garnish with lemon slices and chives and serve with freshly cooked conchiglie.

Serves 4. Makes 750 ml (26 fl oz/3 ½ cups).

Total Cals/Kj: 743/3115	Total fat: 35.9 g
Cals/Kj per portion: 186/779	Fat per portion: 8.9 g
Cals/Kj per cup: 212/890	Fat per cup: 10.3 g

Variation: Use pink salmon or tuna in place of the red salmon.

—— SCAMPI & MUSHROOM ——

2 teaspoons sunflower oil
1 onion, chopped
1 green pepper (capsicum), chopped
1 clove garlic, crushed
225 g (8 oz) button mushrooms, halved
3 tomatoes, peeled, seeded and chopped
175 ml (6 fl oz/¾ cup) fish stock
115 ml (4 fl oz/½ cup) dry white wine
1 tablespoon chopped fresh thyme
salt and freshly ground black pepper
450 g (1 lb) frozen scampi, thawed and drained
1 tablespoon cornflour
fresh thyme, to garnish

In a saucepan, heat oil and cook onion, green pepper (capsicum), and garlic for 5 minutes.

Add the mushrooms, tomatoes, stock, wine, thyme and salt and pepper and mix well. Bring to the boil, cover and simmer gently for 10 minutes, stirring occasionally. Add the scampi and cook for a further 5 minutes. In a bowl, blend the cornflour with 2 tablespoons water and add to the pan.

Bring back to the boil, stirring continuously, until the mixture has thickened. Simmer for 3 minutes. Garnish with thyme and serve with freshly cooked linguine or fettucine.

Serves 6. Makes 1.2 litres (42 fl oz/5¼ cups).

Total Cals/Kj: 857/3607	Total fat: 21.2 g
Cals/Kj per portion: 143/601	Fat per portion: 3.5 g
Cals/Kj per cup: 163/687	Fat per cup: 4.0 g

Variation: Use other seafood such as prawns or cockles in place of the scampi.

—— TUNA & ANCHOVY ——

2 teaspoons olive oil
3 shallots, finely chopped
1 clove garlic, crushed
225 g (8 oz) mushrooms, sliced
175 ml (6 fl oz/¾ cup) fish stock
150 ml (5 fl oz/⅔ cup) dry white wine
200 g (7 oz) can tuna in brine, drained and flaked
100 g (3½ oz) can anchovies in brine, drained and
    chopped
1 tablespoon capers, chopped
salt and freshly ground black pepper
1 tablespoon cornflour
1 tablespoon chopped fresh parsley
fresh parsley, to garnish

In a saucepan, heat the oil and cook the
shallots and garlic for 1 minute. Add the
mushrooms, cover and cook for 5 minutes,
stirring occasionally. Stir in the stock, wine,
tuna, anchovies, capers and salt and pepper
and mix well. Bring to the boil and simmer
gently for 3 minutes, stirring.

In a small bowl, blend the cornflour with
2 tablespoons water and add to the pan.
Bring back to the boil, stirring continuously,
until the mixture has thickened. Simmer for
3 minutes, then stir in the parsley just before
serving. Garnish with parsley and serve with
freshly cooked penne.

Serves 4. Makes 850 ml (30 fl oz/3¾ cups).

Total Cals/Kj: 798/3348   Total fat: 32.7 g
Cals/Kj per portion: 199/837   Fat per portion: 8.1 g
Cals/Kj per cup: 213/893   Fat per cup: 8.7 g

— SMOKED TROUT WITH LIME —

300 g (10 oz) smoked trout fillets
300 ml (10 fl oz/1 ¼ cups) very low fat plain fromage
    frais
4 tablespoons reduced calorie mayonnaise
2 tablespoons horseradish sauce
grated rind and juice of 1 lime
2 tablespoons chopped fresh parsley
salt and freshly ground black pepper
150 g (5 oz) sugar snap peas, diagonally sliced
5 sticks celery, cut into matchstick strips
lime slices and parsley sprigs, to garnish

Skin the trout and discard any bones. Cut
the flesh into small pieces and set aside.

In a large bowl, mix together the fromage
frais, mayonnaise, horseradish sauce, lime
rind, lime juice, parsley and salt and pepper,
until thoroughly combined.

Add the trout, sugar snap peas and celery
and mix well. Garnish with lime slices and
parsley and serve with freshly cooked farfalle
or conchiglie.

Serves 6. Makes 900 ml (32 fl oz/4 cups).

Total Cals/Kj: 878/3693   Total fat: 34.6 g
Cals/Kj per portion: 146/616   Fat per portion: 5.7 g
Cals/Kj per cup: 219/923   Fat per cup: 8.6 g

SPICED SEAFOOD

150 ml (5 fl oz/²⁄₃ cup) fish stock, cooled
150 ml (5 fl oz/²⁄₃ cup) dry white wine
2 tablespoons tomato purée (paste)
1 ½ teaspoons each ground coriander and cumin
1 teaspoon each chilli powder and ground ginger
½ teaspoon turmeric
450 g (1 lb) cooked mixed seafood
2 teaspoons olive oil
1 onion, chopped
1 clove garlic, crushed
1 red pepper (capsicum), sliced
200 g (7 oz) can sweetcorn kernels, drained
salt and freshly ground black pepper
1 tablespoon cornflour
2 tablespoons chopped fresh coriander
coriander sprigs, to garnish

In a bowl, mix together the stock, wine, tomato purée (paste) and spices. Add the seafood and mix well. Cover, chill and leave to marinate for 1 hour. In a saucepan, heat the oil and add the onion, garlic and pepper (capsicum). Cover and cook gently for 10 minutes, stirring occasionally. Add the seafood, marinade, sweetcorn and salt and pepper and mix well. Bring to the boil and simmer gently for 5 minutes, stirring occasionally. In a bowl, blend the cornflour with 2 tablespoons water and add to the pan.

Bring back to the boil, stirring continuously, until the mixture thickens. Simmer for 3 minutes. Stir in the coriander just before serving. Garnish with coriander and serve with freshly cooked tagliatelle or spaghetti.

Serves 6. Makes 1.2 litres (42 fl oz/5 ¼ cups).

Total Cals/Kj: 1000/4213   Total fat: 23.4 g
Cals/Kj per portion: 167/702   Fat per portion: 3.9 g
Cals/Kj per cup: 190/802   Fat per cup: 4.4 g

Note: Buy a pack of mixed seafood or use scampi, prawns and scallops.

COD IN WHITE WINE

45 g (1½ oz/3 tablespoons) half fat spread
2 courgettes (zucchini), diagonally sliced
3 shallots, thinly sliced
45 g (1½ oz/⅓ cup) plain flour
175 ml (6 fl oz/¾ cup) fish stock
175 ml (6 fl oz/¾ cup) dry white wine
2 tablespoons chopped fresh mixed herbs
salt and freshly ground black pepper
450 g (1 lb) cod fillet, skinned and cubed
fresh parsley, to garnish

Preheat the oven to 190C (375F/Gas 5). In a large saucepan, melt the half fat spread over a low heat. Add the courgettes (zucchini) and shallots and cook for 3 minutes.

Stir in the flour and cook for 1 minute, stirring. Remove the pan from the heat and gradually stir in the stock and wine. Bring slowly to the boil, stirring, and continue to cook, stirring, until the mixture thickens.

Add the herbs, salt and pepper and fish and mix gently but thoroughly. Transfer to an ovenproof dish. Cover and cook in the oven for 20-25 minutes, stirring once. Garnish with parsley and serve with freshly cooked spaghetti or linguine.

Serves 4. Makes 1 litre (35 fl oz/4½ cups).

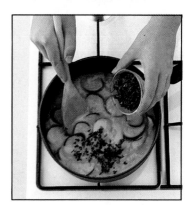

Total Cals/Kj: 870/3648   Total fat: 23.5 g
Cals/Kj per portion: 218/912   Fat per portion: 5.9 g
Cals/Kj per cup: 193/811   Fat per cup: 5.2 g

———— TUNA & CHILLI BEAN ————

175 ml (6 fl oz/ ¾ cup) very low fat plain fromage
    frais
115 ml (4 fl oz/ ½ cup) reduced calorie mayonnaise
1-2 teaspoons chilli powder
2 tablespoons chopped fresh mixed herbs
1 bunch spring onions, cut into 1 cm (½ in) lengths
3 sticks celery, thinly sliced
400 g (14 oz) can tuna in brine, drained and flaked
400 g (14 oz) can red kidney beans, rinsed and
    drained
salt and freshly ground black pepper
fresh parsley, to garnish

In a bowl, mix together the fromage frais,
mayonnaise, chilli powder and herbs.

Add the spring onions, celery, tuna, red
kidney beans and salt and pepper, mixing
well. Chill until ready to serve. Garnish with
parsley and serve with freshly cooked fusilli.

Serves 6. Makes 1.1 litres (38½ fl oz/5 cups).

Total Cals/Kj: 1252/5291   Total fat: 36.2 g
Cals/Kj per portion: 209/882   Fat per portion: 6.0 g
Cals/Kj per cup: 250/1058   Fat per cup: 7.2 g

Variation: Use either red salmon or canned
sardines in place of the tuna.

— SMOKED HADDOCK & CAPER —

450 ml (16 fl oz/2 cups) semi-skimmed milk
1 bay leaf
450 g (1 lb) smoked haddock fillets, skinned
25 g (1 oz/2 tablespoons) half fat spread
1 onion, finely chopped
25 g (1 oz/¼ cup) plain flour
2 tablespoons capers, halved
1 tablespoon chopped fresh chives
salt and freshly ground black pepper
basil sprigs, to garnish

Pour the milk into a large frying pan, add the bay leaf and smoked haddock and bring slowly to the boil. Cover and simmer gently for 15-20 minutes, until the fish is cooked.

Strain the milk into a jug and set aside. Discard the bay leaf, flake the fish, removing any bones, and set aside. In a large saucepan, melt the half fat spread over a low heat. Add the onion and cook gently for 5 minutes, stirring occasionally. Stir in the flour and cook for 1 minute, stirring. Remove the pan from the heat and gradually stir in the reserved milk.

Bring slowly to the boil, stirring, and continue to cook, stirring, until the mixture thickens. Add the flaked fish, capers, chives and salt and pepper and simmer gently for 5 minutes, stirring. Garnish with basil sprigs and serve with freshly cooked paglia e fieno.

Serves 6. Makes 1.1 litres (38½ fl oz/5 cups).

Total Cals/Kj: 811/3433	Total fat: 20.7 g
Cals/Kj per portion: 135/572	Fat per portion: 3.5 g
Cals/Kj per cup: 162/687	Fat per cup: 4.1 g

—— CLAM & COURGETTE ——

2 teaspoons sunflower oil
1 bunch spring onions, cut into 1 cm (½ in) lengths
1 green pepper (capsicum), sliced
115 g (4 oz) mushrooms, sliced
2 courgettes (zucchini), sliced
450 g (1 lb) tomatoes, peeled and finely chopped
4 tablespoons dry sherry
450 g (1 lb) small fresh clams (venus clams), scrubbed
juice of 1 lime
1 tablespoon chopped fresh mixed herbs
salt and freshly ground black pepper
1 tablespoon cornflour

In a large frying pan or wok, heat the oil and cook the spring onions and pepper (capsicum) for 5 minutes.

Add the mushrooms, courgettes (zucchini), tomatoes and sherry and mix well. Bring gently to the boil, cover and simmer for 15 minutes, stirring occasionally. Add the clams, lime juice, herbs and salt and pepper and mix well. Cover and cook for 5 minutes, stirring occasionally. In a small bowl, blend the cornflour with 2 tablespoons water and add to the pan.

Cook, stirring, until the mixture has thickened, then simmer for 3 minutes. Serve with freshly cooked cappellini or spaghetti.

Serves 6. Makes 1250 ml (44 fl oz/5½ cups).

Total Cals/Kj: 602/2531   Total fat: 15.8 g
Cals/Kj per portion: 100/422   Fat per portion: 2.6 g
Cals/Kj per cup: 109/460   Fat per cup: 2.9 g

Note: Before cooking, discard any cracked or open clams. Once the clams have been cooked, discard any unopened ones.

— PINK SALMON & TARRAGON —

25 g (1 oz/2 tablespoons) half fat spread
2 leeks, sliced
1 clove garlic, crushed
25 g (1 oz/¼ cup) plain flour
300 ml (10 fl oz/1¼ cups) semi-skimmed milk
150 ml (5 fl oz/⅔ cup) fish stock
400 g (14 oz) can pink salmon in brine, drained,
 boned and flaked
2 tablespoons chopped fresh tarragon
salt and freshly ground black pepper
tarragon sprigs, to garnish

In a saucepan, melt the half fat spread over a low heat. Add the leeks and garlic, cover and cook for 5 minutes, stirring occasionally.

Stir in the flour and cook for 1 minute, stirring. Remove the pan from the heat and gradually stir in the milk and stock. Bring slowly to the boil, stirring, and continue to cook, stirring, until the mixture thickens.

Add the salmon, tarragon and salt and pepper and simmer gently for 5 minutes, stirring occasionally. Garnish with tarragon sprigs and serve with freshly cooked linguine.

Serves 6. Makes 900 ml (32 fl oz/4 cups).

Total Cals/Kj: 1005/4231   Total fat: 43.3 g
Cals/Kj per portion: 168/705   Fat per portion: 7.2 g
Cals/Kj per cup: 251/1058   Fat per cup: 10.8 g

Variation: Use red salmon or tuna in brine, in place of the pink salmon.

—— PRAWN & YELLOW PEPPER ——

2 yellow peppers (capsicum), halved
2.5 cm (1 in) piece fresh root ginger, peeled and
   finely chopped
1 bunch spring onions, cut into 1 cm (½ in) lengths
350 g (12 oz) cooked, peeled prawns
175 ml (6 fl oz/ ¾ cup) very low fat plain fromage frais
150 ml (5 fl oz/ ⅔ cup) low fat plain yogurt
2 teaspoons finely grated lemon rind
1 tablespoon chopped fresh chives
1 tablespoon chopped fresh parsley
salt and freshly ground black pepper

Preheat grill. Place the peppers (capsicum) on
a grill pan and cook under a medium heat
until the skin blisters.

Place the peppers (capsicum) in a bowl, cover
with cling film and leave to cool. Peel off and
discard the skins, remove and discard the
seeds and cores and cut the flesh into strips.

Place the peppers (capsicum) in a large bowl,
add the ginger, spring onions, prawns,
fromage frais, yogurt, lemon rind, chives,
parsley and salt and pepper and mix well.
Serve with freshly cooked tortiglioni.

Serves 4. Makes 900 ml (32 fl oz/4 cups).

Total Cals/Kj: 666/2827	Total fat: 6.3 g
Cals/Kj per portion: 167/707	Fat per portion: 1.6 g
Cals/Kj per cup: 167/707	Fat per cup: 1.6 g

SARDINE & TOMATO

1 clove garlic
1 onion
115 g (4 oz) mushrooms
1 teaspoon olive oil
400 g (14 oz) can chopped tomatoes
225 g (8 oz) can chopped tomatoes
2 tablespoons chopped fresh mixed herbs
salt and freshly ground black pepper
3 x 120 g (4 oz) cans sardines in brine, drained and
    flaked
basil leaves, to garnish

Finely chop garlic and slice onion and mushrooms. In a saucepan, heat oil and cook garlic, onion and mushrooms for 5 minutes.

Add the tomatoes, herbs and salt and pepper and mix well. Bring to the boil, cover and simmer for 10 minutes, stirring occasionally.

Add the flaked sardines and simmer gently for 2-3 minutes until the fish is heated through. Serve with freshly cooked rigatoni.

Serves 6. Makes 1.1 litres (38½ fl oz/5 cups).

Total Cals/Kj: 841/3534   Total fat: 41.2 g
Cals/Kj per portion: 140/589   Fat per portion: 6.8 g
Cals/Kj per cup: 168/707   Fat per cup: 8.2 g

CURRIED MONKFISH

150 ml (5 fl oz / ⅔ cup) fish stock, cooled
70 ml (2½ fl oz / ⅓ cup) dry white wine
1 tablespoon lemon juice
1 tablespoon curry powder
1 teaspoon each ground cumin, coriander and ginger
350 g (12 oz) monkfish, skinned and cubed
2 teaspoons sunflower oil
1 onion, sliced
1 clove garlic, crushed
1 small red pepper (capsicum), diced
115 g (4 oz) mushrooms, sliced
3 sticks celery, sliced, leaves reserved for garnish
2 courgettes (zucchini), sliced
2 small carrots, sliced
70 g (2½ oz / ½ cup) raisins
2 eating apples, cored, quartered and sliced

Place the stock, wine, lemon juice, curry powder and spices in a bowl and add the fish. Stir gently to coat the fish, cover, chill and leave to marinate for 45 minutes. In a large saucepan, heat the oil, add the vegetables, cover and cook gently for 10 minutes, stirring occasionally. Add the fish, marinade and raisins and stir gently to mix. Bring to the boil and simmer gently for 10 minutes, stirring occasionally.

Add the apples and cook for 5 minutes, stirring occasionally. Garnish with reserved celery leaves and serve with freshly cooked spaghetti or tagliatelle.

Serves 6. Makes 1.5 litres (52½ fl oz/6¾ cups).

Total Cals/Kj: 1000/4225   Total fat: 19.8 g
Cals/Kj per portion: 167/704   Fat per portion: 3.3 g
Cals/Kj per cup: 148/626   Fat per cup: 2.9 g

Variation: Stir in 2 tablespoons reduced fat single (light) cream just before serving.

—— CREAMY TUNA & LEMON ——

175 g (6 oz) frozen peas
400 g (14 oz) can tuna in brine, drained
finely grated rind and juice of 1 lemon
450 ml (16 fl oz/2 cups) very low fat plain fromage
    frais
70 ml (2½ fl oz/⅓ cup) reduced calorie mayonnaise
2 tablespoons chopped fresh parsley
salt and freshly ground black pepper
lemon wedges and salad leaves, to garnish

Cook the peas in a pan of boiling, salted water for 5 minutes. Drain and leave to cool.

Flake the tuna into a bowl. Add the lemon rind, lemon juice, fromage frais, mayonnaise, parsley, salt and pepper and cooked peas and mix gently but thoroughly. Chill in the refrigerator until ready to serve.

Adjust the seasoning just before serving. Garnish with lemon wedges and salad leaves and serve with freshly cooked penne.

Serves 6. Makes 1.1 litres (38½ fl oz/5 cups).

Total Cals/Kj: 1027/4337	Total fat: 28.9 g
Cals/Kj per portion: 171/723	Fat per portion: 4.8 g
Cals/Kj per cup: 205/867	Fat per cup: 5.8 g

Variation: Use canned salmon in place of the tuna, and the finely grated rind and juice of 1 small orange in place of the lemon.

— COD, GARLIC & ROSEMARY —

25 g (1 oz/2 tablespoons) half fat spread
3 shallots, finely chopped
3 cloves garlic, crushed
1 green pepper (capsicum), sliced
25 g (1 oz/¼ cup) plain flour
300 ml (10 fl oz/1¼ cups) fish stock
150 ml (5 fl oz/⅔ cup) dry white wine
2 tablespoons lemon juice
2 teaspoons dried rosemary
450 g (1 lb) cod steaks, skinned and cubed
175 g (6 oz) frozen broad beans
salt and freshly ground black pepper
rosemary sprigs, to garnish

In a large saucepan, melt the half fat spread
over a low heat.

Add the shallots, garlic and pepper
(capsicum) and cook gently for 3 minutes,
stirring. Add flour and cook for 1 minute,
stirring. Remove the pan from the heat and
gradually stir in the stock, wine and lemon
juice. Bring slowly to the boil, stirring, and
continue to cook, stirring, until the mixture
thickens. Preheat oven to 180C (350F/Gas 4).

Add the rosemary, cod, broad beans and salt
and pepper to the saucepan and mix well.
Transfer cod mixture to an ovenproof dish,
cover and cook in the oven for 25 minutes,
stirring once. Garnish with rosemary sprigs
and serve with freshly cooked tagliatelle.

Serves 6. Makes 1.2 litres (42 fl oz/5¼ cups).

Total Cals/Kj: 862/3631   Total fat: 16.8 g
Cals/Kj per portion: 144/605   Fat per portion: 2.8 g
Cals/Kj per cup: 164/692   Fat per cup: 3.2 g

DEVILLED SHRIMPS

2 teaspoons sunflower oil
1 bunch spring onions, cut into 1 cm (½ in) lengths
1 clove garlic, crushed
700 g (1 ½ lb) tomatoes, peeled and finely chopped
2 tablespoons tomato ketchup
2 teaspoons Dijon mustard
1 teaspoon caster sugar
1 teaspoon chilli powder
1 teaspoon ground cumin
juice of 1 lemon
salt and freshly ground black pepper
350 g (12 oz) cooked, peeled shrimps
coriander leaves, to garnish

In a saucepan, heat the oil, add the spring onions and garlic and cook for 5 minutes.

Add the tomatoes, tomato ketchup, mustard, sugar, spices, lemon juice and salt and pepper and mix well. Bring to the boil, cover and simmer for 10 minutes, stirring occasionally.

Uncover and simmer over a higher heat for 5 minutes, until the sauce has thickened. Add the shrimps, mix well and cook for a further 2-3 minutes. Garnish with coriander and serve with freshly cooked linguine.

Serves 4. Makes 950 ml (33 fl oz/4 ¼ cups).

Total Cals/Kj: 722/3046   Total fat: 23.8 g
Cals/Kj per portion: 181/762   Fat per portion: 5.9 g
Cals/Kj per cup: 170/717   Fat per cup: 5.6 g

—— SALMON & WATERCRESS ——

15 g (½ oz/1 tablespoon) half fat spread
2 shallots, finely chopped
1 clove garlic, crushed
175 g (6 oz) watercress
175 ml (6 fl oz/¾ cup) very low fat plain fromage
    frais
150 ml (5 fl oz/⅔ cup) reduced fat single (light)
    cream
1 teaspoon Dijon mustard
salt and freshly ground black pepper
2 x 225 g (8 oz) cans red salmon in brine, drained

In a saucepan, melt the half fat spread, add the shallots, garlic and watercress, reserving 6 sprigs for garnish, and cook for 3 minutes.

Leave to cool. Place the cooled watercress mixture in a blender or food processor. Add the fromage frais, cream, mustard and salt and pepper and blend until smooth. Transfer to a large bowl.

Flake the salmon, removing any bones, and stir into the watercress mixture. Garnish with the reserved watercress and serve with freshly cooked farfalle.

Serves 6. Makes 1 litre (35 fl oz/4½ cups).

Total Cals/Kj: 1166/4887   Total fat: 63.5 g
Cals/Kj per portion: 194/815   Fat per portion: 10.6 g
Cals/Kj per cup: 259/1086   Fat per cup: 14.1 g

——— CLAMS IN WHITE WINE ———

1 small onion, sliced
1 small carrot, sliced
1 bay leaf
6 black peppercorns
300 ml (10 fl oz/1 ¼ cups) dry white wine
25 g (1 oz/2 tablespoons) half fat spread
2 leeks, diagonally sliced
2 carrots, diagonally sliced
175 g (6 oz) button mushrooms
25 g (1 oz/¼ cup) plain flour
150 ml (5 fl oz/⅔ cup) fish stock
1 tablespoon chopped fresh mixed herbs
salt and freshly ground black pepper
450 g (1 lb) small fresh clams (venus clams),
    scrubbed
flat-leaf parsley, to garnish

Place the onion, carrot, bay leaf, peppercorns and wine in a saucepan and bring to the boil. Remove the pan from the heat, cover and set aside to infuse for 20 minutes. Strain the wine into a jug, reserving the wine and discarding the vegetables. In a saucepan, melt the half fat spread over a low heat. Add the leeks, carrots and mushrooms, cover and cook for 8 minutes, stirring occasionally. Add the flour and cook for 1 minute, stirring. Remove from the heat and gradually stir in the flavoured wine and the stock.

Bring slowly to the boil, stirring, and continue to cook, stirring, until the mixture thickens. Add the herbs, salt and pepper and clams and cook for 5 minutes, stirring occasionally. Discard any unopened clams. Garnish with flat-leaf parsley and serve with freshly cooked paglia e fieno or tagliatelle.

Serves 6. Makes 1.3 litres (47 fl oz/6 cups).

Total Cals/Kj: 746/3127   Total fat: 15.1 g
Cals/Kj per portion: 124/521   Fat per portion: 2.5 g
Cals/Kj per cup: 124/521   Fat per cup: 2.5 g

—— SMOKED SALMON & DILL ——

175 g (6 oz) smoked salmon
225 g (8 oz) low fat soft cheese
150 ml (5 fl oz/²⁄₃ cup) very low fat plain fromage frais
3 tablespoons reduced fat single (light) cream
1 small onion, finely chopped
1 tablespoon lemon juice
2 tablespoons chopped fresh dill
salt and freshly ground black pepper
3 tomatoes, peeled and finely chopped
2 sticks celery, finely chopped
dill sprigs and strips of lemon rind, to garnish

Cut the salmon into thin strips and set aside.

Place the soft cheese, fromage frais, cream, onion, lemon juice, dill and salt and pepper in a food processor or blender and blend until the mixture is smooth. Transfer to a large bowl.

Add the smoked salmon, tomatoes and celery and mix lightly. Chill until ready to serve. Adjust the seasoning, garnish and serve with freshly cooked pappardelle.

Serves 6. Makes 900 ml (32 fl oz/4 cups).

Total Cals/Kj: 775/3270	Total fat: 27.4 g
Cals/Kj per portion: 194/817	Fat per portion: 6.8 g
Cals/Kj per cup: 194/817	Fat per cup: 6.8 g

Variation: Replace the smoked salmon with smoked trout, or salmon or tuna in brine.

—MEDITERRANEAN PRAWNS—

2 teaspoons olive oil
1 red pepper (capsicum), sliced
1 yellow pepper (capsicum), sliced
2 courgettes (zucchini), sliced
2 leeks, sliced
3 sticks celery, thinly sliced
2 carrots, diced
2 cloves garlic, crushed
2 beefsteak tomatoes, peeled and finely chopped
150 ml (5 fl oz/⅔ cup) fish stock
1 teaspoon dried oregano
salt and freshly ground black pepper
350 g (12 oz) cooked, peeled prawns
1 tablespoon chopped fresh basil
oregano sprigs, to garnish

In a large frying pan or wok, heat the oil and add the peppers (capsicum), courgettes (zucchini), leeks, celery, carrots and garlic. Cover and cook gently for 10 minutes, stirring occasionally. Add the tomatoes, stock, oregano and salt and pepper and mix well. Cover and cook for 10 minutes, stirring occasionally.

Add the prawns, cover and cook gently for 5 minutes, stirring occasionally. Uncover, increase the heat and cook for 3 minutes, stirring occasionally, until the sauce is thickened. Stir in the basil. Garnish with oregano sprigs and serve with freshly cooked garlic and herb tagliatelle.

Serves 6. Makes 1.3 litres (45½ fl oz/5¾ cups).

Total Cals/Kj: 859/3619   Total fat: 19.9 g
Cals/Kj per portion: 143/603   Fat per portion: 3.3 g
Cals/Kj per cup: 149/629   Fat per cup: 3.5 g

SMOKED TROUT

150 ml (5 fl oz/⅔ cup) semi-skimmed milk
350 g (12 oz) smoked trout fillets, skinned
25 g (1 oz/2 tablespoons) half fat spread
1 onion, finely chopped
25 g (1 oz/¼ cup) plain flour
300 ml (10 fl oz/1¼ cups) fish stock
3 tomatoes, peeled and finely chopped
1 tablespoon chopped fresh dill
1 tablespoon chopped fresh thyme
salt and freshly ground black pepper
lemon slices and thyme sprigs, to garnish

Place the milk and trout in a large saucepan. Bring slowly to the boil, remove from the heat and let stand for 20 minutes.

Drain the fish, reserving the milk. Flake the fish, removing any bones, and set aside to cool. In a saucepan, melt the half fat spread over a low heat. Add the onion and cook for 5 minutes. Stir in the flour and cook for 1 minute, stirring. Remove the pan from the heat and gradually stir in the reserved milk and the stock. Bring slowly to the boil, stirring, and continue to cook, stirring, until the mixture thickens.

Add the flaked fish, tomatoes, herbs and salt and pepper and mix well. Simmer gently for 5 minutes, stirring. Garnish with lemon slices and thyme sprigs and serve with freshly cooked fusilli bucati.

Serves 4. Makes 900 ml (32 fl oz/4 cups).

Total Cals/Kj: 858/3602	Total fat: 30.6 g
Cals/Kj per portion: 215/901	Fat per portion: 7.6 g
Cals/Kj per cup: 215/901	Fat per cup: 7.6 g

——— SALMON & ASPARAGUS———

450 g (1 lb) fresh salmon fillets, skinned and cubed
juice of 1 lemon
1 clove garlic, crushed
175 ml (6 fl oz/ ¾ cup) fish stock, cooled
2 tablespoons dry white wine
1 tablespoon light soy sauce
salt and freshly ground black pepper
2 teaspoons sunflower oil
350 g (12 oz) asparagus, cut into 1 cm (½ in) pieces
1 tablespoon cornflour
1 tablespoon chopped fresh tarragon

In a bowl, mix together the salmon, lemon juice, garlic, stock, wine, soy sauce and salt and pepper. Cover, chill and leave to marinate for 30 minutes. In a large frying pan or wok, heat the oil. Remove the fish from the marinade with a slotted spoon, reserving the marinade, and add the fish to the pan with the asparagus. Stir-fry over a high heat for 2-3 minutes until the fish is just cooked. Blend the cornflour with the marinade and add to the pan with the tarragon.

Bring to the boil over a high heat, stirring continuously, for 1-2 minutes, until the sauce is thickened and glossy. Serve immediately with freshly cooked lasagnette.

Serves 6. Makes 1 litre (35 fl oz/4 ½ cups).

Total Cals/Kj: 1078/4489   Total fat: 12.2 g
Cals/Kj per portion: 179/748   Fat per portion: 2.0 g
Cals/Kj per cup: 239/997   Fat per cup: 2.7 g

TUNA & SWEETCORN

400 g (14 oz) can tuna in brine, drained
200 g (7 oz) can sweetcorn kernels, drained
1 small onion, grated
175 ml (6 fl oz/¾ cup) very low fat plain fromage frais
150 ml (5 fl oz/⅔ cup) low fat plain yogurt
3 tablespoons reduced calorie mayonnaise
1 tablespoon capers, finely chopped
1 teaspoon Dijon mustard
salt and freshly ground black pepper
1 tablespoon chopped fresh parsley
parsley sprigs, to garnish

In a large bowl, mix together the tuna, sweetcorn kernels, onion, fromage frais, yogurt and mayonnaise.

Stir in the capers, mustard, salt and pepper and parsley and mix gently but thoroughly.

Chill in the refrigerator until ready to serve. Adjust the seasoning, garnish with parsley sprigs and serve with freshly cooked fusilli.

Serves 6. Makes 1 litre (35 fl oz/4½ cups).

Total Cals/Kj: 1016/4304
Cals/Kj per portion: 169/717
Cals/Kj per cup: 226/956

Total fat: 19.7 g
Fat per portion: 3.3 g
Fat per cup: 4.4 g

Variation: Place all the ingredients except the sweetcorn in a blender or food processor and blend until smooth. Stir in the sweetcorn.

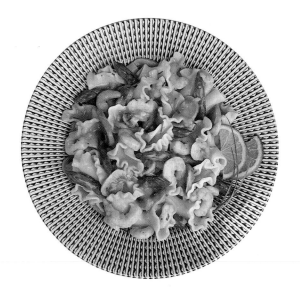

PRAWN & ASPARAGUS

225 g (8 oz) fresh asparagus tips
25 g (1 oz/2 tablespoons) half fat spread
2 shallots, finely chopped
1 clove garlic, crushed
175 g (6 oz) mushrooms, sliced
2.5 cm (1 in) piece fresh root ginger, peeled and
  finely chopped
25 g (1 oz/ ¼ cup) plain flour
300 ml (10 fl oz/1 ¼ cups) fish stock
150 ml (5 fl oz/ ⅔ cup) dry white wine
juice of 1 lime
2 teaspoons soft brown sugar
350 g (12 oz) cooked, peeled prawns
1 tablespoon chopped fresh chives
salt and freshly ground black pepper
lime slices and chives, to garnish

Cook the asparagus tips in a saucepan of
boiling water for 3 minutes. Drain well and
set aside. In a saucepan, melt the half fat
spread over a low heat. Add the shallots,
garlic, mushrooms and ginger and cook for
5 minutes, stirring occasionally. Stir in the
flour and cook for 1 minute, stirring.
Remove the pan from the heat and gradually
stir in the stock and wine. Bring slowly to the
boil, stirring, and continue to cook, stirring,
until the mixture thickens.

Add the lime juice, sugar, asparagus tips and
prawns and simmer gently for 5 minutes,
stirring. Stir in the chives and salt and pepper
and mix well. Garnish with lime slices and
chives and serve with freshly cooked fiorelli.

Serves 6. Makes 1.2 litres (42 fl oz/5 ¼ cups).

Total Cals/Kj: 764/3211	Total fat: 16.0 g
Cals/Kj per portion: 127/535	Fat per portion: 2.7 g
Cals/Kj per cup: 145/612	Fat per cup: 3.0 g

CHINESE-STYLE FISH

225 g (8 oz) can pineapple pieces in fruit juice
150 ml (5 fl oz/⅔ cup) fish stock, cooled
2 tablespoons light soy sauce
2 tablespoons soft brown sugar
2 tablespoons dry sherry
2 tablespoons tomato ketchup
1 teaspoon Chinese five-spice powder
450 g (1 lb) monkfish, skinned and cubed
2 teaspoons olive oil
1 bunch spring onions, cut into 1 cm (½ in) lengths
1 red pepper (capsicum), sliced
1 clove garlic, crushed
200 g (7 oz) can sweetcorn kernels, drained
1 tablespoon cornflour
salt and freshly ground black pepper
spring onions, to garnish

Drain the pineapple, reserving the juice. Chop the pineapple flesh roughly and set aside. Place the pineapple juice in a bowl with the stock, soy sauce, sugar, sherry, tomato ketchup and five-spice powder. Add the monkfish and mix well. Cover, chill and leave to marinate for 1 hour. In a large frying pan or wok, heat the oil. Remove fish from marinade with a slotted spoon, reserving the marinade and add the fish to the pan with the spring onions, pepper (capsicum) and garlic. Stir-fry over a high heat for 3-5 minutes until the fish is just cooked.

Add sweetcorn and pineapple and cook for 1 minute, stirring. Blend cornflour with the marinade and add to the pan with the salt and pepper. Bring to the boil over a high heat, stirring, for 1-2 minutes, until the sauce is thickened and glossy. Garnish with spring onions and serve immediately with freshly cooked tagliatelle.

Serves 6. Makes 1.1 litres (38½ fl oz/5 cups).

Total Cals/Kj: 1120/4753   Total fat: 15.8 g
Cals/Kj per portion: 187/792   Fat per portion: 2.6 g
Cals/Kj per cup: 224/951   Fat per cup: 3.2 g

CRAB & WHITE WINE

1 small onion, sliced
1 small carrot, sliced
½ stick celery, sliced
1 bay leaf
6 black peppercorns
300 ml (10 fl oz/1 ¼ cups) dry white wine
25 g (1 oz/2 tablespoons) half fat spread
4 sticks celery, cut into matchstick strips
1 small onion, finely chopped
25 g (1 oz/¼ cup) plain flour
150 ml (5 fl oz/⅔ cup) fish stock
2 x 170 g (6 oz) cans crab meat, drained
salt and freshly ground black pepper
2 tablespoons chopped fresh parsley
4 tablespoons reduced fat single (light) cream
parsley, to garnish

Place the sliced onion, carrot, celery, bay leaf and peppercorns in a saucepan with the wine and bring to the boil. Remove the pan from the heat, cover and set aside to infuse for 20 minutes. Strain the wine into a jug, reserving the wine and discarding the vegetables. In a saucepan, melt the half fat spread over a low heat. Add the celery and onion. Cover and cook for 10 minutes, stirring occasionally. Stir in the flour and cook for 1 minute, stirring. Remove the pan from the heat and gradually stir in the flavoured wine and stock.

Bring slowly to the boil, stirring, and continue to cook, stirring, until the mixture thickens. Add the crab, salt and pepper and parsley and cook for 5 minutes, stirring occasionally. Remove the pan from the heat and stir in the cream. Garnish with parsley and serve with freshly cooked spaghetti.

Serves 4. Makes 1 litre (35 fl oz/4 ½ cups).

Total Cals/Kj: 772/3247
Cals/Kj per portion: 193/812
Cals/Kj per cup: 172/721

Total fat: 18.8 g
Fat per portion: 4.7 g
Fat per cup: 4.2 g

– SPICY TOMATO & MUSHROOM –

1 teaspoon olive oil
1 bunch spring onions, cut into 1 cm (½ in) lengths
1 clove garlic, crushed
115 g (4 oz) button mushrooms, halved
1 fresh red chilli, seeded and finely chopped
700 g (1½ lb) tomatoes, peeled, seeded and finely
   chopped
150 ml (5 fl oz/⅔ cup) dry white wine
1 teaspoon ground cumin
salt and freshly ground black pepper
lemon and lime slices and coriander leaves, to
   garnish

In a saucepan, heat the oil and cook the
spring onions, garlic, mushrooms and chilli
for 5 minutes, stirring occasionally.

Stir in the tomatoes, wine, cumin and salt
and pepper, mixing well. Bring to the boil,
cover and simmer gently for 15 minutes,
stirring occasionally.

Uncover and simmer for 10 minutes, until
the sauce has thickened. Garnish with lemon
and lime slices and coriander leaves and serve
with freshly cooked linguine.

Serves 2. Makes 700 ml (24½ fl oz/3¼ cups).

Total Cals/Kj: 322/1361   Total fat: 9.4 g
Cals/Kj per portion: 161/681   Fat per portion: 4.7 g
Cals/Kj per cup: 99/419   Fat per cup: 2.9 g

MUSHROOM & GARLIC

25 g (1 oz/2 tablespoons) half fat spread
1 onion, finely chopped
4 cloves garlic, crushed
450 g (1 lb) mushrooms, sliced
25 g (1 oz/¼ cup) plain flour
175 ml (6 fl oz/¾ cup) semi-skimmed milk
115 ml (4 fl oz/½ cup) vegetable stock
salt and freshly ground black pepper
2 tablespoons reduced fat single (light) cream
1 tablespoon chopped fresh parsley
flat-leaf parsley, to garnish

In a large frying pan or wok, melt the half fat spread over a low heat. Add the onion and garlic and cook for 5 minutes.

Add the mushrooms, cover and cook gently for 8 minutes, stirring occasionally. Stir in the flour and cook for 1 minute, stirring. Remove the pan from the heat and gradually stir in the milk and stock. Bring slowly to the boil, stirring, and continue to cook, stirring, until the mixture thickens.

Add the salt and pepper and simmer gently for 3 minutes, stirring. Remove the pan from the heat and stir in the cream and parsley. Garnish with flat-leaf parsley and serve with freshly cooked bucatini.

Serves 4. Makes 900 ml (32 fl oz/4 cups).

Total Cals/Kj: 430/1805   Total fat: 18.8 g
Cals/Kj per portion: 108/451   Fat per portion: 4.7 g
Cals/Kj per cup: 108/451   Fat per cup: 4.7 g

──── STIR-FRIED VEGETABLES ────

1 tablespoon cornflour
175 ml (6 fl oz/¾ cup) vegetable stock
4 tablespoons dry white wine
2 tablespoons light soy sauce
1 tablespoon clear honey
juice of 1 lime
1 teaspoon garam masala
salt and freshly ground black pepper
2 teaspoons sunflower oil
1 red onion, sliced
1 yellow pepper (capsicum), sliced
175 g (6 oz) broccoli flowerets
115 g (4 oz) okra, trimmed and halved
3 carrots, diagonally sliced
115 g (4 oz) mange tout (snow peas)
115 g (4 oz) bean sprouts

In a bowl, blend the cornflour with the stock, wine, soy sauce, honey, lime juice, garam masala and salt and pepper. Set aside. In a large frying pan or wok, heat the oil. Add the onion and pepper (capsicum) and stir-fry over a high heat for 1 minute. Add the broccoli, okra and carrots and stir-fry over a medium heat for 5 minutes. Add the mange tout (snow peas) and bean sprouts and stir-fry for 1 minute.

Add the cornflour mixture and bring to the boil over a high heat, stirring continuously, for 1-2 minutes, until the sauce is thickened and glossy. Serve immediately with freshly cooked linguine.

Serves 4. Makes 1.1 litres (38½ fl oz/5 cups).

Total Cals/Kj: 661/2765   Total fat: 16.4 g
Cals/Kj per portion: 165/691   Fat per portion: 4.1 g
Cals/Kj per cup: 132/553   Fat per cup: 3.3 g

——BROAD BEAN & PARSLEY——

350 g (12 oz) broad beans
25 g (1 oz/2 tablespoons) half fat spread
25 g (1 oz/¼ cup) plain flour
300 ml (10 fl oz/1¼ cups) semi-skimmed milk
150 ml (5 fl oz/⅔ cup) vegetable stock
1 teaspoon mustard powder
salt and freshly ground black pepper
4 tablespoons chopped fresh parsley

Cook the broad beans in a saucepan of boiling water for 10 minutes until tender. Drain and set aside.

In a saucepan, melt the half fat spread over a low heat. Stir in the flour and cook for 1 minute, stirring. Remove the pan from the heat and gradually stir in the milk and stock. Bring slowly to the boil, stirring, and continue to cook, stirring, until the mixture thickens.

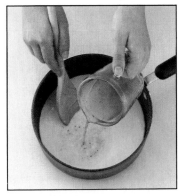

Add the broad beans, mustard powder, salt and pepper and parsley and simmer gently for 5 minutes, stirring. Serve with freshly cooked fusilli bucati.

Serves 4. Makes 800 ml (28 fl oz/3½ cups).

Total Cals/Kj: 630/2661   Total fat: 19.0 g
Cals/Kj per portion: 157/665   Fat per portion: 4.7 g
Cals/Kj per cup: 180/760   Fat per cup: 5.4 g

Note: You can use frozen broad beans if fresh ones are not available.

──RED WINE & MUSHROOM──

2 teaspoons olive oil
4 shallots, sliced
3 sticks celery, finely chopped
350 g (12 oz) button mushrooms
1 clove garlic, crushed
175 ml (6 fl oz/¾ cup) red wine
115 ml (4 fl oz/½ cup) vegetable stock
1 tablespoon chopped fresh rosemary
salt and freshly ground black pepper
1 tablespoon cornflour
rosemary sprigs, to garnish

In a saucepan, heat the oil and add the shallots, celery, mushrooms and garlic.

Cover and cook gently for 10 minutes until the vegetables are soft, stirring occasionally. Add the wine, stock, rosemary and salt and pepper and mix well. In a small bowl, blend the cornflour with 2 tablespoons water and add to the pan.

Bring the mixture to the boil, stirring, and continue to cook, stirring, until the mixture thickens. Simmer for 3 minutes, stirring occasionally. Garnish with rosemary sprigs and serve with freshly cooked tagliatelle.

Serves 4. Makes 850 ml (30 fl oz/3¾ cups).

Total Cals/Kj: 375/1573   Total fat: 13.9 g
Cals/Kj per portion: 94/393   Fat per portion: 3.5 g
Cals/Kj per cup: 100/419   Fat per cup: 3.7 g

— CHUNKY VEGETABLE KORMA —

2 teaspoons sunflower oil
2 onions, sliced
2 cloves garlic, crushed
2.5 cm (1 in) piece fresh root ginger, peeled and
　finely chopped
3 teaspoons curry powder
1 teaspoon each ground cumin and turmeric
4 carrots, sliced
300 g (10 oz) cauliflower flowerets
175 g (6 oz) swede, diced
1 small aubergine (eggplant), diced
55 g (2 oz/¼ cup) sultanas
1 tablespoon plain flour
450 ml (16 fl oz/2 cups) vegetable stock
salt and freshly ground black pepper
150 ml (5 fl oz/⅔ cup) low fat plain yogurt

In a large saucepan, heat the oil and cook the
onions, garlic and ginger for 3 minutes. Add
the curry powder, cumin and turmeric and
cook for 1 minute, stirring. Add the carrots,
cauliflower, swede, aubergine (eggplant) and
sultanas and cook for 5 minutes, stirring. Stir
in the flour and cook for 1 minute, stirring.
Remove the pan from the heat and gradually
stir in the vegetable stock. Bring slowly to the
boil, stirring, and continue to cook, stirring,
until the mixture thickens. Add salt and
pepper and mix well.

Cover and simmer gently for 30-45 minutes
until the vegetables are tender, stirring
occasionally. Remove the pan from the heat
and stir in half of the yogurt. Drizzle with the
remaining yogurt and serve with freshly
cooked conchiglie.

Serves 6. Makes 1.5 litres (53 fl oz/6¾ cups).

Total Cals/Kj: 856/3592　　　Total fat: 21.5 g
Cals/Kj per portion: 143/599　Fat per portion: 3.6 g
Cals/Kj per cup: 127/532　　　Fat per cup: 3.2 g

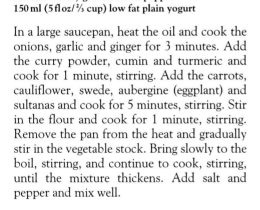

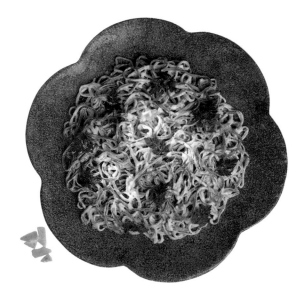

——— GARLIC & HERB ———

2 shallots
4 cloves garlic
175 g (6 oz) medium fat soft cheese
250 ml (9 fl oz/1 cup) very low fat plain fromage frais
150 ml (5 fl oz/⅔ cup) reduced fat single (light) cream
3-4 tablespoons chopped fresh mixed herbs
salt and freshly ground black pepper
chervil sprigs, to garnish

Finely chop the shallots and crush the garlic.

In a bowl, mix together the shallots, garlic and soft cheese and mix well. Stir in the fromage frais and cream. Stir in the mixed herbs and salt and pepper and mix thoroughly. Cover and chill in the refrigerator until ready to serve.

Adjust the seasoning, garnish with chervil sprigs and serve with freshly cooked paglia e fieno or spaghetti.

Serves 4. Makes 600 ml (21 fl oz/2¾ cups).

Total Cals/Kj: 678/2832   Total fat: 40.6 g
Cals/Kj per portion: 170/708   Fat per portion: 10.1 g
Cals/Kj per cup: 246/1030   Fat per cup: 14.8 g

Variation: Place all the ingredients in a blender or food processor and blend until smooth, if preferred.

— THREE PEPPER & TOMATO —

2 teaspoons olive oil
2 leeks, sliced
2 cloves garlic, crushed
1 red, 1 green and 1 yellow pepper (capsicum),
    diced
2 courgettes (zucchini), sliced
450 g (1 lb) tomatoes, peeled and chopped
115 ml (4 fl oz/ ⅓ cup) vegetable stock
4 tablespoons dry white wine
salt and freshly ground black pepper
2 tablespoons chopped fresh basil
basil sprigs, to garnish

In a large frying pan or wok, heat the oil and cook the leeks and garlic for 5 minutes.

Add the peppers (capsicum) and courgettes (zucchini) and cook for 5 minutes, stirring occasionally. Add the tomatoes, stock, wine and salt and pepper and mix well. Bring to the boil, cover and simmer for 15 minutes, stirring occasionally.

Stir in the basil, garnish with basil sprigs and serve with freshly cooked lasagnette.

Serves 6. Makes 1.2 litres (42 fl oz/5 ¼ cups).

Total Cals/Kj: 450/1894   Total fat: 15.6 g
Cals/Kj per portion: 75/316   Fat per portion: 2.6 g
Cals/Kj per cup: 82/344   Fat per cup: 2.8 g

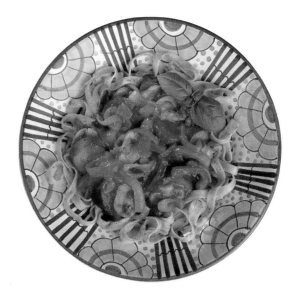

RATATOUILLE

1 large aubergine (eggplant), quartered and sliced
2 teaspoons olive oil
2 onions, sliced
2 cloves garlic, crushed
1 red pepper (capsicum), sliced
1 yellow pepper (capsicum), sliced
1 green pepper (capsicum), sliced
4 courgettes (zucchini), sliced
225 g (8 oz) mushrooms, sliced
400 g (14 oz) can chopped tomatoes
2 tablespoons tomato purée (paste)
salt and freshly ground black pepper
1 tablespoon chopped fresh basil
1 tablespoon chopped fresh parsley
basil sprigs, to garnish

Place the aubergine (eggplant) slices on a plate and sprinkle liberally with salt. Leave for 30 minutes. Rinse, drain thoroughly and pat dry with kitchen paper. In a large saucepan, heat the oil and cook the onions and garlic for 5 minutes. Add the remaining ingredients, except the garnish, and mix well.

Bring to the boil, cover and simmer gently for 30 minutes, stirring occasionally. Uncover for the last 10 minutes of cooking time to thicken the sauce. Serve with freshly cooked garlic and herb tagliatelle.

Serves 6. Makes 1.9 litres (67 fl oz/8½ cups).

Total Cals/Kj: 608/2556   Total fat: 17.9 g
Cals/Kj per portion: 101/426   Fat per portion: 2.9 g
Cals/Kj per cup: 71/301   Fat per cup: 2.1 g

Note: Sprinkling the aubergine (eggplant) with salt extracts the bitter juices.

— CREAMY LEEK & TARRAGON —

45 g (1 ½ oz/3 tablespoons) half fat spread
3 small leeks, diagonally sliced
1 clove garlic, crushed
45 g (1 ½ oz/ ⅓ cup) plain flour
550 ml (20 fl oz/2 ½ cups) semi-skimmed milk
115 g (4 oz) low fat soft cheese
2 tablespoons chopped fresh tarragon
salt and freshly ground black pepper

In a saucepan, melt the half fat spread over a low heat. Add the leeks and garlic, cover and cook gently for 8 minutes, stirring occasionally.

Stir in the flour and cook for 1 minute, stirring. Remove the pan from the heat and gradually stir in the milk. Bring slowly to the boil, stirring, and continue to cook, stirring, until the mixture thickens. Simmer gently for 3 minutes, stirring.

Stir in the soft cheese, tarragon and salt and pepper and heat gently, stirring. Serve with freshly cooked linguine.

Serves 4. Makes 850 ml (30 fl oz/3 ¾ cups).

Total Cals/Kj: 802/3379   Total fat: 36.4 g
Cals/Kj per portion: 201/845   Fat per portion: 9.1 g
Cals/Kj per cup: 214/901   Fat per cup: 9.7 g

— BEAN & LENTIL BOLOGNESE —

1 teaspoon sunflower oil
1 onion, chopped
1 clove garlic, crushed
225 g (8 oz/1 cup) green or brown lentils, rinsed
4 carrots, sliced
225 g (8 oz) mushrooms, sliced
3 sticks celery, sliced
400 g (14 oz) can chopped tomatoes
2 tablespoons tomato purée (paste)
450 ml (16 fl oz/2 cups) vegetable stock
300 ml (10 fl oz/1 ¼ cups) red wine
400 g (14 oz) can each red kidney beans and
    cannellini beans, rinsed and drained
2 teaspoons dried herbes de Provence
salt and freshly ground black pepper
flat-leaf parsley, to garnish

In a large saucepan, heat the oil and cook the onion and garlic for 3 minutes. Add the lentils, carrots, mushrooms and celery and cook for 5 minutes, stirring. Add the tomatoes, tomato purée (paste), stock, wine, beans, herbes de Provence and salt and pepper and mix well.

Bring to the boil, cover and simmer gently for 15 minutes, stirring occasionally. Uncover and simmer for 20-30 minutes, stirring occasionally, until the lentils are tender. Garnish with flat-leaf parsley and serve with freshly cooked spaghetti.

Serves 6. Makes 1.9 litres (67 fl oz/8 ½ cups).

Total Cals/Kj: 1682/7129   Total fat: 15.3 g
Cals/Kj per portion: 280/1188   Fat per portion: 2.6 g
Cals/Kj per cup: 198/839   Fat per cup: 1.8 g

— VEGETABLE & SMOKED TOFU —

1 tablespoon cornflour
300 ml (10 fl oz/1¼ cups) vegetable stock, cooled
2 tablespoons each dark soy sauce and dry sherry
1 tablespoon tomato purée (paste)
½ teaspoon each ground bay leaves and cumin
salt and freshly ground black pepper
2 teaspoons sesame oil
1 bunch spring onions, cut into 2.5 cm (1 in) lengths
2 cloves garlic, crushed
350 g (12 oz) smoked tofu, cut into bite-sized pieces
1 red pepper (capsicum), diced
1 yellow pepper (capsicum), diced
2 courgettes (zucchini), diagonally sliced
175 g (6 oz) baby sweetcorn, halved
3 carrots, cut into matchstick strips
225 g (8 oz) can chick peas, rinsed and drained

In a bowl, blend the cornflour with the stock, soy sauce, sherry, tomato purée (paste), spices and salt and pepper and set aside. In a large frying pan or wok, heat the oil and stir-fry the spring onions and garlic over a high heat for 1 minute. Add the tofu, peppers (capsicum), courgettes (zucchini), baby sweetcorn, carrots and chick peas and stir-fry over a medium heat for 5-8 minutes until the vegetables are just cooked.

Add the cornflour mixture to the pan and bring to the boil over a high heat, stirring continuously, for 1-2 minutes, until the sauce is thickened and glossy. Serve immediately with freshly cooked fusilli.

Serves 6. Makes 1.4 litres (49 fl oz/6¼ cups).

Total Cals/Kj: 1068/4482   Total fat: 36.9 g
Cals/Kj per portion: 178/747   Fat per portion: 6.1 g
Cals/Kj per cup: 171/717   Fat per cup: 5.9 g

— CRISPY SPRING VEGETABLE —

2 teaspoons sunflower oil
1 bunch spring onions, cut into 1 cm (½ in) lengths
1 clove garlic, crushed
2 carrots, cut into matchstick strips
1 small red pepper (capsicum), sliced
2 courgettes (zucchini), cut into matchstick strips
55 g (2 oz) spring greens, roughly chopped
115 g (4 oz) bean sprouts
115 g (4 oz) broccoli flowerets, roughly chopped
1 tablespoon cornflour
300 ml (10 fl oz/1¼ cups) vegetable stock
4 tablespoons brandy
2 tablespoons light soy sauce
salt and freshly ground black pepper
dash of Tabasco sauce
2 tablespoons chopped fresh flat-leaf parsley

In a large frying pan or wok, heat the oil.
Add the spring onions, garlic, carrots and
pepper (capsicum) and stir-fry over a
high heat for 1 minute. Add the courgettes
(zucchini), spring greens, bean sprouts and
broccoli and stir-fry for 5 minutes. In a small
bowl, blend the cornflour with the stock,
brandy and soy sauce.

Add to the pan with the salt and pepper and
bring to the boil over a high heat, stirring
continuously, for 1-2 minutes, until the sauce
is thickened and glossy. Stir in the Tabasco
sauce and parsley and mix well. Serve
immediately with freshly cooked linguine.

Serves 4. Makes 900 ml (32 fl oz/4 cups).

Total Cals/Kj: 577/2404   Total fat: 15.3 g
Cals/Kj per portion: 144/601   Fat per portion: 3.8 g
Cals/Kj per cup: 144/601   Fat per cup: 3.8 g

TOMATO & RED ONION

700 g (1½ lb) tomatoes, peeled and chopped
2 red onions, sliced
1 clove garlic, crushed
150 ml (5 fl oz/⅔ cup) red wine
115 ml (4 fl oz/⅓ cup) vegetable stock
2 tablespoons tomato purée (paste)
2 tablespoons tomato ketchup
2 tablespoons chopped fresh parsley
few drops of Worcestershire sauce
salt and freshly ground black pepper
parsley, to garnish

Place the tomatoes, onions and garlic in a saucepan and mix well.

Add the red wine, vegetable stock, tomato purée (paste), tomato ketchup, parsley, Worcestershire sauce and salt and pepper and mix well. Bring slowly to the boil, cover and simmer gently for 15 minutes, stirring occasionally.

Uncover and simmer for 10 minutes, stirring occasionally, until the sauce is thickened. Garnish with parsley and serve with freshly cooked tortiglioni.

Serves 4. Makes 950 ml (33 fl oz/4¼ cups).

Total Cals/Kj: 384/1620
Cals/Kj per portion: 96/405
Cals/Kj per cup: 90/381

Total fat: 2.8 g
Fat per portion: 0.7 g
Fat per cup: 0.6 g

VEGETABLE CHILLI

225 g (8 oz) swede, diced
4 carrots, sliced
1 onion, sliced
2 leeks, sliced
1 clove garlic, crushed
1 small red pepper (capsicum), diced
225 g (8 oz) baby sweetcorn, halved
400 g (14 oz) can chopped tomatoes
150 ml (5 fl oz/²⁄₃ cup) vegetable stock
4 tablespoons dry white wine
2 tablespoons tomato purée (paste)
2 teaspoons hot chilli powder
salt and freshly ground black pepper
175 g (6 oz) broccoli flowerets
basil sprigs, to garnish

Place the swede, carrots, onion, leeks, garlic, red pepper (capsicum), baby sweetcorn and tomatoes in a saucepan and mix well. Add the vegetable stock, wine, tomato purée (paste), chilli powder and salt and pepper and mix well.

Bring slowly to the boil, cover and simmer for 25 minutes, stirring occasionally. Uncover, add the broccoli and simmer for 10 minutes, stirring occasionally, until the sauce is thickened. Garnish with basil sprigs and serve with freshly cooked fusilli.

Serves 6. Makes 1.7 litres (60 fl oz/7 ¾ cups).

Total Cals/Kj: 595/2502
Cals/Kj per portion: 99/417
Cals/Kj per cup: 77/323

Total fat: 8.9 g
Fat per portion: 1.5 g
Fat per cup: 1.1 g

——— FRESH GARDEN HERB ———

1 bunch spring onions
25 g (1 oz) watercress
1 clove garlic
300 ml (10 fl oz/1 ¼ cups) very low fat plain fromage frais
150 ml (5 fl oz/⅔ cup) reduced calorie mayonnaise
150 ml (5 fl oz/⅔ cup) low fat plain yogurt
juice of 1 lime
1 teaspoon Dijon mustard
4 tablespoons chopped fresh mixed herbs
salt and freshly ground black pepper
lemon and lime slices and watercress, to garnish

Cut the spring onions into 1 cm (½ in) pieces. Chop the watercress and crush the garlic.

Place the spring onions, watercress and garlic in a large bowl. Add the fromage frais, mayonnaise and yogurt and mix well. Stir in the lime juice, mustard, herbs and salt and pepper and mix thoroughly.

Cover and chill in the refrigerator until ready to serve. Adjust the seasoning, garnish with lemon and lime slices and watercress and serve with freshly cooked fiorelli.

Serves 4. Makes 750 ml (26 fl oz/3 ½ cups).

Total Cals/Kj: 750/3131	Total fat: 45.7 g
Cals/Kj per portion: 187/783	Fat per portion: 11.4 g
Cals/Kj per cup: 214/894	Fat per cup: 13.0 g

— MUSHROOM, HERB & SHERRY —

25 g (1 oz/2 tablespoons) half fat spread
1 small onion, finely chopped
225 g (8 oz) mushrooms, thinly sliced
225 g (8 oz) brown-cap or chestnut mushrooms,
    thinly sliced
25 g (1 oz/¼ cup) plain flour
150 ml (5 fl oz/⅔ cup) vegetable stock
150 ml (5 fl oz/⅔ cup) dry sherry
3 tomatoes, peeled and finely chopped
2 tablespoons chopped fresh mixed herbs
salt and freshly ground black pepper
parsley sprigs, to garnish

In a frying pan, melt the half fat spread over a
low heat. Add onion and cook for 1 minute.

Add the mushrooms, cover and cook gently
for 8 minutes until soft, stirring occasionally.
Stir in the flour and cook for 1 minute,
stirring. Remove the pan from the heat and
gradually stir in the stock and sherry. Bring
slowly to the boil, stirring, and continue to
cook, stirring, until the mixture thickens.
Simmer for 3 minutes, stirring occasionally.

Add the tomatoes, herbs and salt and pepper
and heat through. Garnish with parsley sprigs
and serve with freshly cooked tagliatelle.

Serves 4. Makes 950 ml (33 fl oz/4¼ cups).

Total Cals/Kj: 493/2065   Total fat: 13.8 g
Cals/Kj per portion: 123/516   Fat per portion: 3.4 g
Cals/Kj per cup: 116/486   Fat per cup: 3.2 g

CHICK PEA & TOMATO

1 onion
2 cloves garlic
175 g (6 oz) button mushrooms
400 g (14 oz) can chopped tomatoes
400 g (14 oz) can chick peas, rinsed and drained
115 ml (4 fl oz/ ½ cup) vegetable stock
2 tablespoons ruby port
1 tablespoon tomato purée (paste)
1 teaspoon dried rosemary
½ teaspoon cayenne pepper
salt and freshly ground black pepper
rosemary sprigs, to garnish

Finely chop the onion, crush the garlic and halve the mushrooms.

Place the onion, garlic and mushrooms in a large saucepan. Add the tomatoes, chick peas, stock, port, tomato purée (paste), rosemary, cayenne pepper and salt and pepper and mix well.

Bring to the boil, cover and simmer gently for 30 minutes, stirring occasionally. Garnish with rosemary sprigs and serve with freshly cooked conchiglie.

Serves 4. Makes 1 litre (35 fl oz/4 ½ cups).

Total Cals/Kj: 483/2043	Total fat: 8.9 g
Cals/Kj per portion: 121/511	Fat per portion: 2.2 g
Cals/Kj per cup: 107/454	Fat per cup: 1.9 g

Note: For a thicker sauce, blend 1 tablespoon cornflour with 2 tablespoons water, add to pan and cook, stirring, for 3 minutes.

—SWEET PEPPER & AUBERGINE—

2 aubergines (eggplant), cut into large cubes
2 red peppers (capsicum), diced
2 yellow peppers (capsicum), diced
2 cloves garlic, crushed
1 bunch spring onions, cut into 1 cm (½ in) lengths
175 ml (6 fl oz/¾ cup) tomato juice
225 g (8 oz) can chopped tomatoes
2 tablespoons chopped fresh mixed herbs
few drops Tabasco sauce
salt and freshly ground black pepper
oregano leaves, to garnish

Preheat the oven to 180C (350F/Gas 4). Place the aubergine (eggplant) cubes on a plate and sprinkle liberally with salt.

Leave to stand for 30 minutes. Rinse, drain thoroughly and pat dry with kitchen paper. Place the aubergines (eggplant), peppers (capsicum), garlic and spring onions in an ovenproof casserole and mix well. Add the tomato juice, tomatoes, herbs, Tabasco sauce and salt and pepper and mix well.

Cover and cook in the oven for 45 minutes, stirring occasionally. Garnish with oregano leaves and serve with freshly cooked pipe rigate or rigatoni.

Serves 6. Makes 1.2 litres (42 fl oz/5¼ cups).

Total Cals/Kj: 391/1670   Total fat: 5.7 g
Cals/Kj per portion: 65/278   Fat per portion: 0.9 g
Cals/Kj per cup: 71/304   Fat per cup: 1.0 g

SPICY MIXED BEAN

25 g (1 oz/2 tablespoons) half fat spread
2 leeks, sliced
1 clove garlic, crushed
4 carrots, sliced
1 green pepper (capsicum), sliced
25 g (1 oz/ ¼ cup) plain flour
300 ml (10 fl oz/1 ¼ cups) vegetable stock
150 ml (5 fl oz/ ⅔ cup) semi-skimmed milk
400 g (14 oz) can each red kidney beans and chick
   peas, rinsed and drained
175 g (6 oz) frozen broad beans
1 teaspoon each ground coriander and cumin
½ teaspoon each ground allspice and cayenne pepper
salt and freshly ground black pepper
coriander, to garnish

In a large saucepan, melt the half fat spread over a low heat. Add the leeks, garlic, carrots and pepper (capsicum) and cook for 5 minutes, stirring. Add the flour and cook for 1 minute, stirring. Remove the pan from the heat and gradually stir in the stock and milk. Bring slowly to the boil, stirring, and continue to cook, stirring, until the mixture thickens.

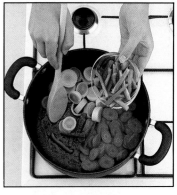

Add the kidney beans, chick peas, broad beans, spices and salt and pepper and mix well. Bring back to the boil, cover and simmer for 30 minutes, stirring occasionally. Garnish with coriander and serve with freshly cooked conchiglie.

Serves 6. Makes 1.3 litres (45½ fl oz/5¾ cups).

Total Cals/Kj: 1107/4675   Total fat: 26.8 g
Cals/Kj per portion: 184/779   Fat per portion: 4.5 g
Cals/Kj per cup: 192/813   Fat per cup: 4.6 g

ORIENTAL CABBAGE

1 tablespoon cornflour
175 ml (6 fl oz/¾ cup) vegetable stock, cooled
3 tablespoons dry sherry
3 tablespoons light soy sauce
2 tablespoons white wine vinegar
2 tablespoons soft brown sugar
1 teaspoon ground ginger
1 teaspoon ground coriander
salt and freshly ground black pepper
2 teaspoons sunflower oil
8 spring onions, cut into 1 cm (½ in) lengths
2 cloves garlic, crushed
1 yellow pepper (capsicum), sliced
1 red pepper (capsicum), sliced
350 g (12 oz) red cabbage, shredded
150 g (5 oz) bean sprouts

In a small bowl, blend the cornflour with the stock, sherry, soy sauce, vinegar, sugar, spices and salt and pepper and set aside. In a large frying pan or wok, heat the oil and stir-fry the spring onions, garlic and peppers (capsicum) for 1 minute over a high heat. Add the cabbage and stir-fry for 3 minutes.

Add the bean sprouts and cook for 1 minute. Add the cornflour mixture and bring to the boil over a high heat, stirring continuously, for 1-2 minutes, until the sauce is thickened and glossy. Serve immediately with freshly cooked lasagnette.

Serves 6. Makes 1 litre (35 fl oz/4½ cups).

Total Cals/Kj: 595/2509   Total fat: 14.4 g
Cals/Kj per portion: 99/418   Fat per portion: 2.4 g
Cals/Kj per cup: 132/558   Fat per cup: 3.2 g

NAPOLETANA

2 teaspoons olive oil
2 cloves garlic, crushed
3 sticks celery, finely chopped
1 kg (2 lb) tomatoes, peeled and finely chopped
1 tablespoon tomato purée (paste)
1 tablespoon chopped fresh basil
1 teaspoon caster sugar
1 bay leaf
salt and freshly ground black pepper
2 tablespoons freshly grated Parmesan cheese
basil sprigs, to garnish

In a saucepan, heat the oil and cook the garlic and celery for 5 minutes.

Add the tomatoes, tomato purée (paste), basil, sugar, bay leaf and salt and pepper and mix well. Cover and bring slowly to the boil, stirring, then simmer gently for 10 minutes, stirring occasionally.

Uncover and cook for 10-15 minutes, stirring occasionally. Remove and discard the bay leaf. Garnish with basil sprigs, sprinkle with Parmesan cheese and serve with freshly cooked pappardelle.

Serves 4. Makes 800 ml (28 fl oz/3½ cups).

Total Cals/Kj: 451/1905   Total fat: 23.3 g
Cals/Kj per portion: 113/476   Fat per portion: 5.8 g
Cals/Kj per cup: 129/544   Fat per cup: 6.6 g

SUMMER STIR-FRY

1 tablespoon cornflour
150 ml (5 fl oz/⅔ cup) vegetable stock
115 ml (4 fl oz/½ cup) tomato juice
4 tablespoons dry sherry
2 tablespoons each soy sauce and tomato ketchup
1 teaspoon each ground ginger and cumin
2 teaspoons sesame oil
1 onion, sliced
1 red and 1 green pepper (capsicum), sliced
175 g (6 oz) baby sweetcorn, halved
115 g (4 oz) broccoli flowerets
2 carrots, cut into matchstick strips
2 sticks celery, sliced, leaves reserved for garnish
1 fresh green chilli, seeded and finely chopped
115 g (4 oz) mange tout (snow peas)
2 tomatoes, peeled and finely chopped

In a bowl, blend the cornflour with the stock, tomato juice, sherry, soy sauce, tomato ketchup, ginger and cumin and set aside. In a large frying pan or wok, heat the oil. Add the onion, peppers (capsicum), sweetcorn, broccoli, carrots, celery and chilli and stir-fry over a high heat for 3 minutes. Add the mange tout (snow peas) and stir-fry for 1 minute. Add the cornflour mixture and bring to the boil over a high heat, stirring continuously, for 1-2 minutes, until the sauce is thickened and glossy.

Stir in the tomatoes and heat through. Garnish with the reserved celery leaves and serve with freshly cooked linguine.

Serves 6. Makes 1.4 litres (49 fl oz/6 ¼ cups).

Total Cals/Kj: 945/3996   Total fat: 16.3 g
Cals/Kj per portion: 157/666   Fat per portion: 2.7 g
Cals/Kj per cup: 151/639   Fat per cup: 2.6 g

──PROVENÇAL VEGETABLE──

2 teaspoons olive oil
1 onion, chopped
2 cloves garlic, crushed
2 leeks, sliced
400 g (14 oz) can chopped tomatoes
150 ml (5 fl oz/⅔ cup) vegetable stock
225 g (8 oz) French beans, halved
225 g (8 oz) fresh or frozen broad beans
3 carrots, sliced
1 tablespoon each chopped fresh basil and parsley
salt and freshly ground black pepper
115 g (4 oz) pitted black olives, halved
flat-leaf parsley, to garnish

In a saucepan, heat the oil and cook the onion and garlic for 3 minutes.

Add the leeks, tomatoes, stock, French beans, broad beans, carrots, basil, parsley and salt and pepper and mix well. Bring slowly to the boil, cover and simmer for 15 minutes, stirring occasionally.

Uncover and simmer for 10 minutes. Add the olives and heat through. Garnish with flat-leaf parsley and serve with freshly cooked penne rigate.

Serves 6. Makes 1.3 litres (45½ fl oz/5¾ cups).

Total Cals/Kj: 705/2954   Total fat: 25.7 g
Cals/Kj per portion: 117/492   Fat per portion: 4.3 g
Cals/Kj per cup: 123/514   Fat per cup: 4.5 g

– SPANISH ONION & MUSHROOM –

25 g (1 oz/2 tablespoons) half fat spread
2 Spanish onions, sliced
1 clove garlic, crushed
350 g (12 oz) mushrooms, sliced
25 g (1 oz/¼ cup) plain flour
175 ml (6 fl oz/¾ cup) vegetable stock
115 ml (4 fl oz/½ cup) Madeira
2 tablespoons tomato purée (paste)
2 teaspoons Dijon mustard
½ teaspoon ground bay leaves
salt and freshly ground black pepper
1 tablespoon chopped fresh parsley
flat-leaf parsley, to garnish

In a saucepan, melt the half fat spread over a low heat.

Add the onions, garlic and mushrooms, cover and cook gently for 10 minutes, stirring occasionally. Add the flour and cook for 1 minute, stirring. Remove the pan from the heat and gradually stir in the stock and Madeira. Bring slowly to the boil, stirring, and continue to cook, stirring, until the mixture thickens.

Add the tomato purée (paste), mustard, ground bay leaves and salt and pepper and simmer gently for 5 minutes, stirring. Stir in the parsley. Garnish with flat-leaf parsley and serve with freshly cooked fusilli.

Serves 4. Makes 950 ml (33 fl oz/4¼ cups).

Total Cals/Kj: 530/2220   Total fat: 13.8 g
Cals/Kj per portion: 132/555   Fat per portion: 3.4 g
Cals/Kj per cup: 125/522   Fat per cup: 3.2 g

—BEAN & SWEETCORN CHILLI—

2 teaspoons sunflower oil
2 onions, sliced
2 cloves garlic, crushed
1-2 teaspoons hot chilli powder
1 teaspoon ground cumin
1 teaspoon ground coriander
3 sticks celery, sliced, leaves reserved for garnish
175 g (6 oz) mushrooms, sliced
150 ml (5 fl oz/⅔ cup) vegetable stock
2 x 200 g (7 oz) cans sweetcorn kernels, drained
400 g (14 oz) can each borlotti beans and red kidney
    beans, rinsed and drained
400 g (14 oz) can chopped tomatoes
2 tablespoons tomato purée (paste)
salt and freshly ground black pepper

In a large saucepan, heat the oil and cook the onions and garlic for 5 minutes. Add the chilli powder, cumin, coriander, celery and mushrooms and cook for 5 minutes, stirring occasionally.

Add the stock, sweetcorn kernels, borlotti beans, kidney beans, tomatoes, tomato purée (paste) and salt and pepper and mix well. Bring slowly to the boil, cover and simmer for 30 minutes, stirring occasionally. Garnish with the reserved celery leaves and serve with freshly cooked tagliatelle.

Serves 6. Makes 1.7 litres (60 fl oz/7¾ cups).

Total Cals/Kj: 1256/5327   Total fat: 23.1 g
Cals/Kj per portion: 209/888   Fat per portion: 3.8 g
Cals/Kj per cup: 162/687   Fat per cup: 2.9 g

— SWEET & SOUR VEGETABLES —

2 tablespoons cornflour
150 ml (5 fl oz/⅔ cup) vegetable stock, cooled
150 ml (5 fl oz/⅔ cup) unsweetened pineapple juice
4 tablespoons white wine vinegar
3 tablespoons each tomato ketchup and soy sauce
2 tablespoons each clear honey and dry sherry
1 teaspoon ground ginger
2 teaspoons sunflower oil
225 g (8 oz) button onions, quartered
175 g (6 oz) baby sweetcorn, halved
175 g (6 oz) broccoli flowerets
175 g (6 oz) button mushrooms
4 sticks celery, sliced
2 carrots, sliced
1 small green pepper (capsicum), diced

In a bowl, blend the cornflour with the stock, pineapple juice, vinegar, tomato ketchup, soy sauce, honey, sherry and ginger and set aside. In a large frying pan or wok, heat the oil and cook the button onions for 5 minutes. Add the sweetcorn, broccoli, mushrooms, celery, carrots and green pepper (capsicum) and stir-fry for 6-8 minutes.

Place the cornflour mixture in a small saucepan. Bring slowly to the boil, stirring, and continue to cook, stirring, until the mixture thickens. Simmer for 2 minutes. Pour over the vegetables and mix well. Simmer for 2 minutes, stirring occasionally. Serve with freshly cooked linguine.

Serves 6. Makes 1.3 litres (45½ fl oz/5¾ cups).

Total Cals/Kj: 768/3244	Total fat: 15.6 g
Cals/Kj per portion: 128/541	Fat per portion: 2.6 g
Cals/Kj per cup: 133/564	Fat per cup: 2.7 g

——— QUICK SPICED TOMATO ———

1 onion
115 g (4 oz) mushrooms
1 clove garlic
400 g (14 oz) can chopped tomatoes
115 ml (4 fl oz/ ½ cup) tomato juice
115 ml (4 fl oz/ ½ cup) vegetable stock
1 tablespoon tomato ketchup
2 teaspoons dried mixed herbs
½ teaspoon ground cumin
salt and freshly ground black pepper
basil sprigs, to garnish

Finely chop the onion and mushrooms and crush the garlic. Place in a pan and add the tomatoes, mixing well.

Stir in the tomato juice, stock, tomato ketchup, mixed herbs, cumin and salt and pepper and mix well.

Bring slowly to the boil, stirring. Simmer gently, uncovered, for 10 minutes, stirring occasionally. Garnish with basil sprigs and serve with freshly cooked conchiglie.

Serves 2. Makes 650 ml (23 fl oz/3 cups).

Total Cals/Kj: 167/710   Total fat: 2.2 g
Cals/Kj per portion: 83/355   Fat per portion: 1.1 g
Cals/Kj per cup: 56/237   Fat per cup: 0.7 g

—— SPRING ONION & GARLIC ——

2 teaspoons olive oil
350 g (12 oz) spring onions, cut into 1 cm (½ in)
   lengths
4 cloves garlic, crushed
½ fresh red chilli, seeded and finely chopped
450 g (1 lb) tomatoes, peeled, seeded and finely
   chopped
4 tablespoons dry sherry
salt and freshly ground black pepper
1 tablespoon chopped fresh basil
lemon slices and spring onion strips, to garnish

In a saucepan, heat the oil and cook the spring onions, garlic and chilli for 5 minutes, stirring occasionally.

Add the tomatoes, sherry, salt and pepper and basil and mix well. Bring slowly to the boil, stirring, then cover and simmer gently for 10 minutes, stirring occasionally.

Uncover and simmer for a further 10 minutes, stirring occasionally, until the sauce has thickened. Garnish with lemon slices and spring onion strips and serve with freshly cooked linguine.

Serves 3. Makes 700 ml (24 ½ fl oz/3 ¼ cups).

Total Cals/Kj: 341/1431   Total fat: 13.3 g
Cals/Kj per portion: 114/477   Fat per portion: 4.4 g
Cals/Kj per cup: 105/440   Fat per cup: 4.0 g

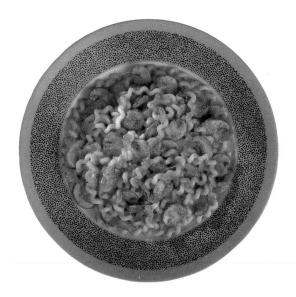

—MUSHROOM & RED PEPPER—

1 teaspoon olive oil
3 shallots, chopped
2 cloves garlic, crushed
3 red peppers (capsicum), diced
150 ml (5 fl oz/ ⅔ cup) vegetable stock
4 tablespoons dry white wine
1 teaspoon ground coriander
1 teaspoon caster sugar
1 teaspoon white wine vinegar
salt and freshly ground black pepper
15 g (½ oz/1 tablespoon) half fat spread
300 g (10 oz) chestnut mushrooms, sliced
coriander leaves, to garnish

In a saucepan, heat the oil and cook shallots, garlic and peppers (capsicum) for 5 minutes.

Add the stock, wine, ground coriander, sugar, vinegar and salt and pepper and mix well. Cover and cook for 5 minutes until the peppers (capsicum) are soft. Remove the pan from the heat and leave to cool. Place the mixture in a food processor or blender and blend until smooth. Set aside. In a saucepan, melt the half fat spread over a low heat. Add the mushrooms, cover and cook gently for 10 minutes, stirring occasionally.

Stir in the pepper (capsicum) sauce and mix well. Heat gently to warm through. Garnish with coriander leaves and serve with freshly cooked fusilli.

Serves 4. Makes 900 ml (32 fl oz/4 cups).

Total Cals/Kj: 383/1603	Total fat: 15.4 g
Cals/Kj per portion: 96/401	Fat per portion: 3.8 g
Cals/Kj per cup: 96/401	Fat per cup: 3.8 g

CRISP GREEN VEGETABLE

300 ml (10 fl oz/1¼ cups) very low fat plain fromage
  frais
4 tablespoons reduced calorie mayonnaise
4 tablespoons Greek yogurt
1 clove garlic, crushed
2 tablespoons chopped fresh mixed herbs
salt and freshly ground black pepper
1 bunch spring onions, cut into 1 cm (½ in) lengths
1 green pepper (capsicum), chopped
175 g (6 oz) cucumber, halved and sliced
115 g (4 oz) sugar snap peas or mange tout (snow
  peas), halved
85 g (3 oz) small broccoli flowerets
mint sprigs, to garnish

In a bowl, mix together the fromage frais,
mayonnaise, yogurt, garlic, herbs and salt
and pepper. Add the spring onions, pepper
(capsicum) and cucumber and mix well.

Stir in the sugar snap peas or mange tout
(snow peas) and broccoli, mixing thoroughly.
Cover and chill until ready to serve. Adjust
the seasoning, garnish with mint sprigs and
serve with freshly cooked conchiglie.

Serves 6. Makes 1 litre (35 fl oz/4½ cups).

Total Cals/Kj: 566/2373   Total fat: 25.4 g
Cals/Kj per portion: 94/395   Fat per portion: 4.2 g
Cals/Kj per cup: 126/527   Fat per cup: 5.6 g

—WILD MUSHROOM & THYME—

1 teaspoon sunflower oil
1 small onion, finely chopped
1 clove garlic, crushed
175 g (6 oz) oyster mushrooms, sliced
175 g (6 oz) shiitake mushrooms, sliced
175 ml (6 fl oz/ ¾ cup) vegetable stock
4 tablespoons dry sherry
4 tomatoes, peeled and finely chopped
1 tablespoon chopped fresh thyme
salt and freshly ground black pepper
thyme leaves, to garnish

In a saucepan, heat the oil and cook the onion and garlic for 5 minutes. Add the mushrooms, stock and sherry and mix well.

Stir in the tomatoes, thyme and salt and pepper and mix well. Bring slowly to the boil, stirring, then cover and simmer gently for 15 minutes, stirring occasionally.

Uncover and simmer for a further 10 minutes, stirring occasionally, until the sauce thickens. Garnish with thyme leaves and serve with freshly cooked fiorelli.

Serves 2. Makes 650 ml (23 fl oz/3 cups).

Total Cals/Kj: 248/1043	Total fat: 7.2 g
Cals/Kj per portion: 124/521	Fat per portion: 3.6 g
Cals/Kj per cup: 83/348	Fat per cup: 2.4 g

CARROT & COURGETTE

2 teaspoons sesame oil
2 leeks, sliced
1 clove garlic, crushed
450 g (1 lb) courgettes (zucchini), sliced
450 g (1 lb) carrots, cut into matchstick strips
2.5 cm (1 in) piece fresh root ginger, peeled and
    finely chopped
115 g (4 oz) ready-to-eat dried apricots, chopped
1 tablespoon cornflour
300 ml (10 fl oz/1¼ cups) vegetable stock
2 tablespoons dark soy sauce
2 tablespoons dry sherry
juice of 1 lime
salt and freshly ground black pepper
chervil sprigs, to garnish

In a large frying pan or wok, heat the oil.
Add the leeks, garlic, courgettes (zucchini),
carrots and ginger and stir-fry over a high
heat for 5 minutes. Add the apricots and mix
well. In a small bowl, blend the cornflour
with the stock, soy sauce, sherry and lime
juice and add to the pan with the salt and
pepper.

Bring to the boil over a high heat, stirring
continuously, for 1-2 minutes, until the sauce
is thickened and glossy. Garnish with chervil
sprigs and serve immediately with freshly
cooked penne rigate.

Serves 6. Makes 1.3 litres (45½ fl oz/5¾ cups).

Total Cals/Kj: 695/2921   Total fat: 15.6 g
Cals/Kj per portion: 116/487   Fat per portion: 2.6 g
Cals/Kj per cup: 121/508   Fat per cup: 2.7 g

——— TOMATO, BASIL & OLIVE ———

1 teaspoon olive oil
2 shallots, finely chopped
1 clove garlic, crushed
400 g (14 oz) can chopped tomatoes
225 g (8 oz) can chopped tomatoes
150 ml (5 fl oz / ⅔ cup) dry vermouth or dry white
  wine
2 tablespoons tomato ketchup
salt and freshly ground black pepper
115 g (4 oz) pitted black olives, halved
3 tablespoons chopped fresh basil
basil sprigs, to garnish

In a saucepan, heat the oil and cook the
shallots and garlic for 5 minutes.

Add the tomatoes, vermouth or wine,
tomato ketchup and salt and pepper and mix
well. Bring to the boil, cover and simmer for
15 minutes, stirring occasionally. Uncover
and boil for a further 5-10 minutes, stirring
occasionally, until the sauce is thickened.

Add the olives and basil and mix well.
Garnish with basil sprigs and serve with
freshly cooked farfalle.

Serves 3. Makes 700 ml (24½ fl oz/3¼ cups).

Total Cals/Kj: 466/1958   Total fat: 16.0 g
Cals/Kj per portion: 155/653 Fat per portion: 5.3 g
Cals/Kj per cup: 143/602   Fat per cup: 4.9 g

—— RED LENTIL & PARSLEY ——

2 teaspoons sunflower oil
2 leeks, sliced
1 clove garlic, crushed
2 carrots, thinly sliced
1 red or green pepper (capsicum), diced
175 g (6 oz) mushrooms, sliced
400 g (14 oz) can chopped tomatoes
550 ml (20 fl oz/2 ½ cups) vegetable stock
300 g (10 oz/1 ¼ cups) split red lentils
salt and freshly ground black pepper
4 tablespoons chopped fresh parsley
parsley sprigs, to garnish

In a large saucepan, heat the oil and cook the leeks and garlic for 5 minutes.

Add the carrots, pepper (capsicum), mushrooms, tomatoes, stock, lentils and salt and pepper and mix well. Bring slowly to the boil, stirring, then cover and simmer gently for 30-45 minutes, stirring occasionally, until the lentils are cooked.

Add the parsley and mix well. Garnish with parsley sprigs and serve with freshly cooked spaghetti or tagliatelle.

Serves 6. Makes 1.5 litres (53 fl oz/6 ¾ cups).

Total Cals/Kj: 1318/5585   Total fat: 18.0 g
Cals/Kj per portion: 220/931   Fat per portion: 3.0 g
Cals/Kj per cup: 195/827   Fat per cup: 2.6 g

CHEESE & ONION

25 g (1 oz/2 tablespoons) half fat spread
1 onion, sliced
1 red onion, sliced
25 g (1 oz/¼ cup) plain flour
300 ml (10 fl oz/1¼ cups) semi-skimmed milk
150 ml (5 fl oz/⅔ cup) vegetable stock
1 tablespoon chopped fresh chives
175 g (6 oz/1½ cups) reduced fat Cheddar cheese,
   grated
salt and freshly ground black pepper
chopped fresh chives, to garnish

In a saucepan, melt the half fat spread over a low heat. Add the onions, cover and cook gently for 10 minutes, stirring occasionally.

Stir in the flour and cook for 1 minute, stirring. Remove the pan from the heat and gradually stir in the milk and stock. Bring slowly to the boil, stirring, and continue to cook, stirring, until the mixture thickens. Simmer gently for 3 minutes.

Remove the pan from the heat and stir in the chives, cheese and salt and pepper, mixing well. Garnish with chopped chives and serve with freshly cooked tagliatelle.

Serves 4. Makes 850 ml (30 fl oz/3¾ cups).

Total Cals/Kj: 898/3763	Total fat: 42.9 g
Cals/Kj per portion: 224/941	Fat per portion: 10.7 g
Cals/Kj per cup: 239/1003	Fat per cup: 11.4 g

EGG & BACON

1 small onion and 1 small carrot, sliced
½ stick celery, sliced
1 bay leaf
6 black peppercorns
300 ml (10 fl oz/1 ¼ cups) semi-skimmed milk
25 g (1 oz/2 tablespoons) half fat spread
2 shallots, finely chopped
85 g (3 oz) streaky bacon, diced
25 g (1 oz/¼ cup) plain flour
150 ml (5 fl oz/⅔ cup) vegetable stock
4 hard-boiled eggs, chopped
4 tomatoes, peeled and finely chopped
salt and freshly ground black pepper
2 tablespoons reduced fat single (light) cream
1 tablespoon chopped fresh parsley
flat-leaf parsley, to garnish

Place the onion, carrot, celery, bay leaf and peppercorns in a saucepan with the milk and bring slowly to the boil. Remove the pan from the heat, cover and leave to infuse for 20 minutes. Strain the milk into a jug, reserving the milk and discarding the vegetables. In a saucepan, melt the half fat spread over a low heat. Add the shallots and bacon, cover and cook gently for 8 minutes, stirring occasionally. Stir in the flour and cook for 1 minute, stirring. Remove the pan from the heat and gradually stir in the flavoured milk and stock.

Bring slowly to the boil, stirring, and continue to cook, stirring, until the mixture thickens. Add the eggs, tomatoes and salt and pepper and simmer gently for 5 minutes. Remove the pan from the heat and stir in the cream and parsley. Garnish with flat-leaf parsley and serve with conchiglie.

Serves 6. Makes 1.1 litres (38½ fl oz/5 cups).

Total Cals/Kj: 1209/5045   Total fat: 85.2 g
Cals/Kj per portion: 202/841 Fat per portion: 14.2 g
Cals/Kj per cup: 242/1009   Fat per cup: 17.0 g

CAULIFLOWER CHEESE

1 small onion, sliced
1 small carrot, sliced
1 bay leaf
6 black peppercorns
300 ml (10 fl oz/1 ¼ cups) semi-skimmed milk
300 g (10 oz) small cauliflower flowerets
45 g (1 ½ oz/3 tablespoons) half fat spread
45 g (1 ½ oz/⅓ cup) plain flour
150 ml (5 fl oz/⅔ cup) vegetable stock
1 teaspoon mustard powder
salt and freshly ground black pepper
55 g (2 oz/½ cup) reduced fat Cheddar cheese, grated
55 g (2 oz/½ cup) reduced fat Red Leicester cheese, grated
cress, to garnish

Place the onion, carrot, bay leaf and peppercorns in a saucepan with the milk and bring slowly to the boil. Remove the pan from the heat, cover and leave to infuse for 20 minutes. Strain the milk into a jug, reserving the milk and discarding the vegetables. In a saucepan of boiling water, cook the cauliflower flowerets until just tender. Drain and set aside. In a saucepan, melt the half fat spread over a low heat. Stir in the flour and cook for 1 minute, stirring. Remove the pan from the heat and gradually stir in the flavoured milk and stock.

Bring slowly to the boil, stirring, and continue to cook, stirring, until the mixture thickens. Add the cauliflower, mustard powder and salt and pepper and simmer for 5 minutes. Remove from the heat and stir in the cheese, reserving a little for garnish. Garnish with the reserved cheese and the cress and serve with freshly cooked bucatini.

Serves 6. Makes 1.1 litres (38½ fl oz/5 cups).

Total Cals/Kj: 872/3655   Total fat: 44.3 g
Cals/Kj per portion: 145/609   Fat per portion: 7.4 g
Cals/Kj per cup: 174/731   Fat per cup: 8.9 g

—— CHEESE & CUCUMBER ——

225 g (8 oz/1 cup) low fat soft cheese
200 ml (7 fl oz/¾ cup) very low fat plain fromage frais
4 tablespoons reduced calorie mayonnaise
4 cloves garlic
4 tablespoons chopped fresh mixed herbs
salt and freshly ground black pepper
225 g (8 oz) cucumber, quartered and sliced
lemon slices and tarragon sprigs, to garnish

Place the soft cheese, fromage frais and mayonnaise in a food processor or blender.

Crush the garlic cloves and add to the blender. Purée the mixture until smooth. Transfer the mixture to a bowl and add the herbs and salt and pepper and mix well. Stir in the cucumber, mixing well.

Cover and chill in the refrigerator until ready to serve. Adjust the seasoning, garnish with lemon slices and tarragon sprigs and serve with freshly cooked fusilli.

Serves 4. Makes 750 ml (26 fl oz/3½ cups).

Total Cals/Kj: 612/2561   Total fat: 31.4 g
Cals/Kj per portion: 153/640   Fat per portion: 7.8 g
Cals/Kj per cup: 175/732   Fat per cup: 8.9 g

—— CHEESE & BROCCOLI ——

350 g (12 oz) broccoli flowerets
25 g (1 oz/2 tablespoons) half fat spread
25 g (1 oz/¼ cup) plain flour
150 ml (5 fl oz/⅔ cup) semi-skimmed milk
150 ml (5 fl oz/⅔ cup) vegetable stock
salt and freshly ground black pepper
115 g (4 oz) reduced fat Cheddar cheese, grated

Steam the broccoli over a pan of boiling water for 4-5 minutes, until tender. Leave to cool slightly, then place in a food processor or blender with 4 tablespoons water and blend until almost smooth. Set aside.

In a saucepan, melt the half fat spread over a low heat. Stir in the flour and cook for 1 minute, stirring. Remove from the heat and gradually add the milk and stock. Bring slowly to the boil, stirring, and continue to cook, stirring, until the mixture thickens.

Add the broccoli purée and salt and pepper and simmer gently for 5 minutes, stirring. Remove the pan from the heat and stir in the cheese, mixing well. Serve with freshly cooked fiorelli.

Serves 4. Makes 850 ml (30 fl oz/3¾ cups).

Total Cals/Kj: 664/2780	Total fat: 33.3 g
Cals/Kj per portion: 166/695	Fat per portion: 8.3 g
Cals/Kj per cup: 177/741	Fat per cup: 8.9 g

SMOKED SALMON & EGG

2 eggs
350 g (12 oz/1 ½ cups) low fat soft cheese
175 ml (6 fl oz/ ¾ cup) low fat plain yogurt
2 shallots, finely chopped
½ teaspoon paprika
1 tablespoon chopped fresh dill
175 g (6 oz) smoked salmon, cut into strips
salt and freshly ground black pepper
lime slices and flat-leaf parsley, to garnish

Hard-boil the eggs in a pan of boiling water for 10 minutes. Plunge the eggs into cold water and allow to cool. Shell the eggs, put into a bowl and mash with a fork.

Put the soft cheese, yogurt, shallots, paprika and dill into a bowl and mix thoroughly. Add the mashed eggs and stir well.

Stir in the smoked salmon and salt and pepper and mix well. Cover and chill until ready to serve. Adjust the seasoning, garnish with lime slices and flat-leaf parsley and serve with freshly cooked tagliatelle.

Serves 6. Makes 900 ml (32 fl oz/4 cups).

Total Cals/Kj: 1028/4317
Cals/Kj per portion: 171/719
Cals/Kj per cup: 257/1079

Total fat: 47.2 g
Fat per portion: 7.8 g
Fat per cup: 11.8 g

—————— CHEESE, HAM & LEEK ——————

25 g (1 oz/2 tablespoons) half fat spread
350 g (12 oz) leeks, sliced
25 g (1 oz/ ¼ cup) plain flour
300 ml (10 fl oz/1 ¼ cups) vegetable stock
150 ml (5 fl oz/ ⅔ cup) semi-skimmed milk
115 g (4 oz) lean cooked smoked ham, diced
salt and freshly ground black pepper
115 g (4 oz/1 cup) reduced fat Red Leicester cheese,
   grated
2 tablespoons chopped fresh chives
rosemary sprigs, to garnish

In a saucepan, melt the half fat spread. Add leeks, cover and cook for 10 minutes. Add the flour and cook for 1 minute, stirring.

Remove the pan from the heat and gradually stir in the stock and milk. Bring slowly to the boil, stirring, and continue to cook, stirring, until the mixture thickens. Add the ham and salt and pepper and simmer gently for 5 minutes, stirring occasionally.

Remove the pan from the heat, stir in the cheese and chives and mix well. Garnish with rosemary sprigs and serve with freshly cooked tortiglioni.

Serves 6. Makes 950 ml (33 fl oz/4 ¼ cups).

Total Cals/Kj: 765/3209   Total fat: 37.8 g
Cals/Kj per portion: 127/535   Fat per portion: 6.3 g
Cals/Kj per cup: 180/755   Fat per cup: 8.9 g

—— BLUE CHEESE & SAGE ——

4 sticks celery
1 clove garlic
115 g (4 oz/ ½ cup) blue Stilton cheese
300 ml (10 fl oz/1 ¼ cups) very low fat plain fromage
frais
150 ml (5 fl oz/ ⅔ cup) low fat plain yogurt
juice of 1 lemon
1-2 tablespoons chopped fresh sage
salt and freshly ground black pepper
sage leaves, to garnish

Finely chop the celery sticks and crush the
garlic. Crumble the Stilton or chop it finely.

Place the celery, garlic and Stilton in a large
bowl. Add the fromage frais and yogurt and
mix well. Stir in the lemon juice, sage and salt
and pepper and mix well. Cover and chill in
the refrigerator until ready to serve.

Adjust the seasoning, garnish with sage leaves
and serve with freshly cooked linguine.

Serves 4. Makes 750 ml (26 fl oz/3 ½ cups).

Total Cals/Kj: 763/3197   Total fat: 43.5 g
Cals/Kj per portion: 191/799   Fat per portion: 10.8 g
Cals/Kj per cup: 218/913   Fat per cup: 12.4 g

Note: Blue cheese is quite salty, so be careful
when seasoning this sauce.

EGG & WATERCRESS

25 g (1 oz/2 tablespoons) half fat spread
1 small onion, finely chopped
2 cloves garlic, crushed
115 g (4 oz) watercress, chopped
25 g (1 oz/¼ cup) plain flour
300 ml (10 fl oz/1¼ cups) vegetable stock
150 ml (5 fl oz/⅔ cup) semi-skimmed milk
3 hard-boiled eggs, finely chopped
salt and freshly ground black pepper
1 tablespoon chopped fresh mixed herbs
watercress sprigs and celery leaves, to garnish

In a saucepan, melt the half fat spread over a low heat. Add the onion, garlic and watercress and cook gently for 3 minutes.

Add the flour and cook for 1 minute, stirring. Remove the pan from the heat and gradually stir in the stock and milk. Bring slowly to the boil, stirring, and continue to cook, stirring, until the mixture thickens.

Add the eggs, salt and pepper and herbs and simmer for 3 minutes, stirring. Garnish with watercress sprigs and celery leaves and serve with freshly cooked penne rigate.

Serves 6. Makes 800 ml (28 fl oz/3½ cups).

Total Cals/Kj: 651/2725   Total fat: 38.6 g
Cals/Kj per portion: 108/454   Fat per portion: 6.4 g
Cals/Kj per cup: 186/778   Fat per cup: 11.0 g

—— FETA CHEESE & SPINACH ——

1 kg (2 lb) fresh spinach leaves
2 cloves garlic, crushed
2 shallots, finely chopped
juice of ½ lemon
¼ teaspoon dried thyme
¼ teaspoon grated nutmeg
salt and freshly ground black pepper
225 g (8 oz/2 cups) feta cheese
oregano leaves, to garnish

Wash the spinach leaves and place in a saucepan. Cover and cook for 1-2 minutes until just wilted. Leave to cool. Place the spinach in a food processor or blender and purée until smooth.

Add the garlic, shallots, lemon juice, thyme, nutmeg and salt and pepper and blend until well combined. Transfer the spinach mixture to a saucepan and bring slowly to the boil. Simmer gently for 5 minutes, stirring.

Crumble the feta cheese and stir into the sauce just before serving. Garnish with oregano and serve with freshly cooked fusilli.

Serves 6. Makes 750 ml (26 fl oz/3 ½ cups).

Total Cals/Kj: 841/3485   Total fat: 53.8 g
Cals/Kj per portion: 140/581   Fat per portion: 8.9 g
Cals/Kj per cup: 240/996   Fat per cup: 15.4 g

Variation: Use 450 g (1 lb) frozen spinach, in place of the fresh spinach. Defrost and purée as with the fresh spinach.

──── SMOKED CHEESE & CHIVE ────

25 g (1 oz/2 tablespoons) half fat spread
1 bunch spring onions, cut into 1 cm (½ in) lengths
2 courgettes (zucchini), diced
25 g (1 oz/¼ cup) plain flour
250 ml (9 floz/1 cup) semi-skimmed milk
250 ml (9 floz/1 cup) vegetable stock
salt and freshly ground black pepper
2 tablespoons chopped fresh chives
115 g (4 oz/1 cup) smoked Cheddar cheese, grated
flat-leaf parsley, to garnish

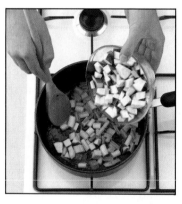

In a saucepan, melt the half fat spread over a low heat. Add the spring onions and courgettes (zucchini), cover and cook gently for 10 minutes, stirring occasionally.

Stir in the flour and cook for 1 minute, stirring. Remove the pan from the heat and gradually stir in the milk and stock. Bring slowly to the boil, stirring, and continue to cook, stirring, until the mixture thickens.

Add the salt and pepper and chives and simmer gently for 3 minutes, stirring. Remove the pan from the heat and stir in the cheese, mixing well. Garnish with flat-leaf parsley and serve with freshly cooked lasagnette.

Serves 6. Makes 800 ml (28 floz/3½ cups).

Total Cals/Kj: 756/3156   Total fat: 45.3 g
Cals/Kj per portion: 126/526   Fat per portion: 7.5 g
Cals/Kj per cup: 216/902   Fat per cup: 12.9 g

INDEX